Hans J. Ullmann
Evamaria Ullmann

Spaniels

Everything about Breeding, Care, Nutrition, and Diseases

Translated by Helgard Niewisch, D.V.M.

With Color Photographs by Outstanding Animal Photographers and Drawings by Sepp Arnemann

D1045863

BARRON'S

Woodbury, New York • London • Toronto • Sydney

First English language edition published in 1982 by Barron's Educational Series, Inc.
© 1980 by Gräfe and Unzer GmbH, Munich, West Germany

The title of the German book is *Spaniels*.

All inquiries should be addressed to:
Barron's Educational Series, Inc.
113 Crossways Park Drive
Woodbury, New York 11797

Library of Congress Catalog Card No. 82-1737
International Standard Book No. 0-8120-2424-9

Library of Congress Cataloging in Publication Data
Ullmann, Hans-Jochen.
    Spaniels: Everything about breeding, care, nutrition, and diseases.
    Translation of: Spaniels.
    Bibliography: p. 68.
    Includes index.
    1. Spaniels. I. Ullmann, Evamaria. II. Title.
SF429.S7U4413   636.7′52   82-1737
ISBN 0-8120-2424-9   AACR2

Front cover: Three Cocker Spaniels: tricolor, orange-white, and blue-ticked; Beatrice Dillis, breeder.
Inside back cover: Retriever spaniel with pheasant.

Photographs
Animal/Thompson: page 9; page 20, lower right and lower left; back cover, lower left.
Schmidecker: inside front cover; page 19; page 20, upper right and upper left.
Ullmann: front cover; inside back cover; back cover, upper right, upper left, and lower right; pages 10, 45, 46, 63; page 64, upper right, upper left, and lower right.

Contents

Spaniels

A Word Up Front

This much is certain: You are an animal lover, like dogs, and have a special interest in spaniels.

Perhaps you intend to acquire a spaniel soon; perhaps you already own one but would like to increase your knowledge regarding the latest findings by behavioral researchers, veterinarians, and breeders. This book about spaniels answers questions you may have with respect to the acquisition, raising, and proper care and feeding of this type of dog. It offers information about diseases and illnesses and introduces all breeds in the spaniel family.

We feel that it is important to discuss not only the happy aspects of owning a spaniel, but also the sometimes less desirable points. In order to avoid potential mistakes, we consider it mandatory to point out possible disadvantages, deficiencies, and problems of this breed.

As photographers of animals, as well as Cocker Spaniel owners, we have had extensive contacts with spaniel fanciers over a time span of many years. We have encountered family pets and have met dogs belonging to bachelors and to single ladies, in addition to dogs living in kennels. We have had most informative discussions with owners and breeders on the seemingly endless topic "spaniels." We have included these experiences in this book. We feel that, aside from necessary theories, practical tips derived from experience are of greatest help to those seeking advice.

Special thanks go to all those who have helped with manuscript and illustrations: Beatrice Dillis and her daughter, owners of the Cocker Spaniel kennels "Vom Munchner Kindl," in Gerold near Garmisch; Ilse Bachmann in Murnsee near Bad Heilbrunn, who enabled us to photograph her cocker bitch giving birth to puppies (Plate 6); Mr. Hiller from Penzing, who belongs to a handful of forest rangers still training Cocker Spaniels for hunting and continues to take them roving through his particular forest territory. We were permitted to photograph his dogs retrieving game birds. And last, but not least, we thank Sepp Arnemann, the creator of the amusing and informative spaniel illustrations.

Now a special word to children is in order.

Dear young spaniel friend:

You, too, ought to read this book, especially if you already own a spaniel, or if you wish you did!

Spaniels really like children, and they can make excellent pets, provided one knows how to handle them properly. If you want a loyal friend, you must make sure that your dog truly enjoys being with you—and your dog will feel really comfortable only when you allow him to follow his own nature. It is important that you study carefully what your spaniel wants, what he is able to do, and what his needs are. All of this—and much more—you can learn from this book. With this knowledge you will surely succeed in making your spaniel your best friend. He will thank you by being loyal and affectionate.

We wish all our readers much success in their wish to live harmoniously with their dogs.

Evamaria Ullmann
Hans J. Ullmann

Considerations Before You Buy

Is a Spaniel the Right Dog for You?

Before you make the final decision to buy a spaniel, be sure to learn as much as possible about the nature, care, and grooming of this type of dog. When you want to buy a car, for example, you make sure to gather as much information as you can about its fuel needs, its care, and its operation. However, a word of caution: Although you may profit by taking a car on a test drive, a short test run with a prospective dog will not tell you enough about the many special attributes of this particular breed, because you are dealing with a living being, which is always more complex than even the most advanced technical machinery.

Please make use of this informative book so that you and your family will know in advance what life will be like with a new spaniel as a potential member of the family. Discuss with each other whether this particular breed will truly fit your needs and match your interests. After you have bought the dog, it will be too late for such considerations.

Also, take into account that you are embarking on a long life together. A spaniel has a life span of approximately 12–14 years. (We have even seen a 16-year-old spaniel in surprisingly good shape.) Perhaps you underestimate the time and effort required to groom his coat. In that case you may be better off with a dog of a short-haired breed, which is easier to groom. Perhaps you would prefer a watchdog rather than a playful, affectionate dog. In that case a German Shepherd or Doberman may be your best bet.

After careful consideration, if you have decided to acquire a spaniel, please know in advance what type of shelter, and where, will be available when you are away from home on business or decide to take a vacation. Unfortunately you cannot take your dog along on all your trips, and you may not have the good fortune to have a friend or neighbor who will take good care of your pet. The only solution may be to look for a reputable kennel, which may or may not present problems for an especially sensitive dog—for example, he may refuse his food.

One more thing you ought to know before acquiring a dog: Do not buy a puppy *without all necessary shots,* and do take your new pet to a veterinarian to receive proper vaccinations and a good checkup. The veterinarian will tell you when to return for booster shots.

Essential Conditions for Keeping a Spaniel

To ensure the most harmonious relationship between dog and owner and to avoid disappointments later on, all future owners of spaniels should be aware of the most important conditions necessary for the care of such a dog. These include the living quarters and daily habits of the owner, as well as his or her occupation. We would like to point out, however, that, regardless of the type of residence (whether you are single or married, with or without children, rent an apartment or own a home), a spaniel is adaptable to almost any type of living arrangements, provided that he has

Considerations Before You Buy

sufficient space to express his barely suppressible, inherent exuberance.

We would, however, advise against living quarters in densely populated urban areas, unless you are close to an area where your dog can be allowed to run. A backyard is preferable, but it cannot be a substitute for the intensive daily schedule of exercise that a spaniel requires and that he can develop to its fullest potential only when you accompany him. You become his "pack leader."

If you live in a small apartment, or if opportunities for the dog to run are limited, you had better decide on a smaller type of spaniel. For example, Cavalier King Charles Spaniels are smaller, and therefore their natural inclination to move about and run is less pronounced.

Estimate on devoting about 2 hours daily to your "hobby," your dog (Figure 1), and allocate much patience on your part for care and training. We consider these minimum requirements, and every dog owner should be prepared to meet them. A spaniel seems to need somewhat more of everything than dogs of other breeds. Here is a list of ten of the most important requirements which a potential owner should be able to fulfill:

1. Have the necessary knowledge and understanding to gain the respect of your dog as his "pack leader."
2. Do not show your puppy that you feel anxious or nervous. Do not speak too loud or be too rough.
3. Do not become a "dictator"; instead be a loving owner, though one who will not diverge from consistent training rules because of begging.

4. Do not be a fanatic when it comes to keeping everything neat.
5. Show your children how to handle the dog properly, and advise them of all applicable rules (p. 22).
6. Do not expect your dog to spend 8 hours daily alone.
7. Take your dog for a walk for a minimum of 1 hour (2 hours are better), rain or shine!
8. Feed your dog a healthful, balanced, not too-calorie-rich diet.
9. Have several friends, relatives, or neighbors who will care for your dog when you are on a trip away from home.

Figure 1   *A most important consideration before you purchase: Will you have sufficient spare time for your dog?*

Plate 1   (above) *American Cocker Spaniel
(left) and Sussex Spaniel
(below) Irish Water Spaniel (left)
and Clumber Spaniel*

10. Be prepared to add to your monthly budget fixed costs of about $30.00 (not counting annual license fees, liability insurance, and veterinary fees) for the dog.

If you can satisfy at least the first three and the last five requirements (and if your landlord does not have a "no pets" policy), you may then enter the hallowed circle of qualified spaniel owners.

Figure 2   *The decision to get a male spaniel entails much patience on your dog walks.*

However, if you don't fare as well on the above test, especially if you cannot satisfy requirements 6, 7, and 10, we urge you to refrain from buying a puppy of this breed. Please consider another pet (for example, a canary or goldfish). But even to those who

qualify according to the above ten important points, we say: Only when you are absolutely certain that getting a spaniel means not only joy but also responsibility and some concessions on the part of you and your family—only then should you really decide on the purchase.

Choices Regarding the Dog

Male or Female?
Potential owners find themselves confronted with the same question as future parents: boy or girl?

This important problem, which parents generally must let fate decide, may be solved by the spaniel owner according to his or her choice. There really is no pressing reason why one sex should be preferable to the other. Therefore we tend to advise you to follow your own preference.

Some people claim that female dogs prefer male owners and male dogs prefer female owners, but there exists no research to bear this out. (Our Cocker Spaniel Amigo, for example, did not differentiate between the two of us when it came time to dole out his favors.) Neither can the claim be substantiated that female dogs are basically more affectionate than male dogs. There are as many aggressive female dogs as there are peaceful male dogs. And, finally, spaniels are true individuals and must be treated as such.

To choose a male dog means: You will need more patience when you walk your dog (Figure 2). The male needs sufficient time to sniff around. He raises his leg

Plate 2   *English Springer Spaniel, German breeder*

often, thus marking his territory. When he follows the scent of a female in heat, you need patience and understanding of his restless behavior, which is dominated by his instinct for procreation. He will settle down after a few days.

To choose a female dog means: You must be aware that the dog will be in heat for a few days twice a year. (See "When Your Dog Is in Heat," p. 30.) If you do not want a new litter, you must watch the female dog carefully during this period. We do not recommend contraceptive hormone injections on a regular basis because frequent injections may cause endocrine imbalances that may affect the dog's health adversely. Particularly persistent male dogs may be kept at a distance with certain deodorant sprays. Despite these helpful measures, however, you have to count on suitors following your female dog around.

Do not choose a female just to share the experience of her giving birth to a litter. We urge you to leave this to qualified breeders who have been endorsed by the various dog clubs and associations. There are many of those—and even more puppies.

Male or female dog: You can readily see that both patience and understanding are needed in equal measure for either one.

Puppy or Grown Dog?
The answer to this question too is yours alone. The advantage of choosing a puppy lies in watching him grow. The owner can experience great joy and happiness in seeing his pet develop from a tiny creature taking his first awkward and unsure steps into an almost all-knowing, life-time companion. But raising a puppy also requires a good measure of effort, time, and patience.

The advantage of choosing a grown dog lies primarily in satisfying the unselfish wish to provide a home. There are many abandoned dogs yearning for an owner to care for them lovingly. Newspaper ads and the sad, longing eyes of animals in a shelter give testimony to the need to find new owners. You can often find purebred spaniels among these dogs. You will undoubtedly bring happiness not only to the animal but also to yourself by giving an abandoned dog a new lease on life. Often such a dog rewards his owner with a particularly strong loyalty and devotion, thus showing his gratitude for being rescued from loneliness. After a short period of adaptation, the grown dog will quickly become accustomed to you and your habits.

Purebred or Mixed-Breed Spaniel?
When a purebred spaniel with a long pedigree is not absolutely necessary for some reason, and when an owner does not intend to exhibit his or her dog at dog shows, a mixed-breed spaniel can be entirely satisfying (for example, a Cocker-Poo). We must emphasize, however, that a certain risk is involved here, as there is at the roulette wheel. Betting on a dog of mixed parentage, you can be in for quite a surprise when the adorable puppy grows up. It is unpredictable whether he will turn into a very large dog, or whether he may become especially intelligent. Even experts in the field of purebred dogs have to admit that mixed dogs frequently develop remarkable intelligence.

Spaniels

When and Where Should You Purchase Your Dog?

The answer to the question "when" really depends on the correct age of the puppy. This means that you cannot plan ahead on an exact date of purchase (as for a birthday present, for example).

The best time to purchase a puppy is when the litter is 8–10 weeks old. A younger puppy still needs the care and warmth provided by the mother. Puppies 8–10 weeks old are no longer whelps; they have been weaned and have learned to take solid food from a bowl. When a change in ownership occurs, there will be few problems of significance regarding the puppy's feeding. How to feed a puppy correctly can be seen on the chart indicating proper weight and calories (p. 35).

The answer to the question "where" can be more difficult. When looking for a spaniel puppy, which belongs to one of the most popular breeds, the enormous array of possibilities can be confusing and bewildering. There are offers from breeders, pet stores, animal shelters, newspaper ads, and so on.

Although some of these offers may be tempting, take the time for a close look at the animals. Carefully check the shelter or other source; note the condition of the litter and, if possible, the mother. Is the litter healthy and wormfree, and has it had all its shots? (See "Health Problems—Diseases and Their Signs," p. 48.) If you want a truly purebred spaniel, ask for its pedigree (registration papers).

When the ancestors of a purebred are known and registered by a registered kennel club, the purity of the desired breed is documented and certified (Figure 3). There are local, state, and national kennel organizations.

Figure 3   *If you want to be sure about quality, you will do best to buy from a recommended registered spaniel kennel.*

If you have tentatively decided by now on a particular puppy, do not buy him immediately. Check whether the puppy suffers from a particular anxiety syndrome (see "Behaviorally Disturbed Dogs," p. 62), which indicates an irreversible behavioral defect, beginning at about the puppy's sixth week. Squat about 6 feet from the puppy,

Considerations Before You Buy

hold out your hand, and talk to him in a low, friendly voice. An animal that shows interest by observing you, or even approaching you with curiosity in order to establish some contact, is reacting in a normal fashion. Should the animal retreat, showing signs of fear or anxiety, or try to hide somewhere, there is evidence of an irreversible behavioral defect. Do not believe salespersons who claim that such behavior lies within the normal range for small dogs.

If the puppy of your choice has successfully passed this little test, revisit him in a few days. Talk to him, play with him a little, and pet him so that he can gradually become used to you. In this way you will help the dog to adapt more easily to the change in environment.

Most breeders and pet-store owners make an honest effort to provide expert care for their animals in order to ultimately find suitable owners for them. However, there are also those among them who are unscrupulous and to whom a dog is nothing but a profit-making object. "Use caution when purchasing a dog," advise reputable dog breeders, and we cannot emphasize too strongly the importance of this caveat. In addition, we offer three important tips:

- Never buy a dog from a catalogue. The poor animals sold in this way, knocked about in crates and cartons, may well have suffered damage through handling and transportation and may even exhibit severe emotional disturbances.
- Avoid the so-called "dog factories" of the large commercial breeders, who always seem to have an unusually large supply of dogs, frequently of many different breeds. Look for smaller breeders recommended by a kennel club. There are also conscientiously conducted pet stores, including those in large department stores, that will gladly provide you with a puppy of your choice from a recognized breeder.

- Do not be fooled by offers of "unusual opportunity" or "special sales." The really basic question is, which type of spaniel would you like to own? To make it easier to decide, we have provided brief descriptions of the various types of breeds within the spaniel family. Basically all spaniels are sporting dogs with more or less ability to retrieve and "flush" (scare) game birds into the air. A few breeds mixed with Asian-type breeds have been excluded from the list but still belong to the general category "spaniels."

The types described are all recognized, proven pure breeds. To make uniform judging possible, the chief international kennel organization, which includes all national dog associations, has established standardized norms for the appearance of each breed, and we describe these here in a brief summary.

Outline of Pure Spaniel Breeds

Definitions of Important Terms

Certain terms are specific for the discussion of dogs. Here is a list of definitions for words sometimes used with reference to spaniels.

Markings: Color distribution of the dog's hair coat.
Black and tan: Typical color combination.
Feathering: Hair fringes at the back of the hind legs.
Fangs: The dog's mouth, with jaws, lips, and cavity.
Clipping: Shortening of the tail in some spaniel breeds, originally done to avoid tangling in the brush during the hunt.
Stripping: Careful removal of hair overgrowth and of loose, shed hair.

Outline of Sporting (Hunting) Spaniels

Brittany Spaniel

This dog originated in the United States and is also very popular in France. It was bred from a mixture of dogs with a predominantly setter line, and has developed into a setter-type spaniel. This dog is used for duck and rabbit hunting and is known as the fastest spaniel for the land hunt. The Brittany Spaniel is a courageous hunter, of great persistence and endurance. His general nature, however, is gentle. He is midsize, gets along well with children, is an excellent watchdog, and is, therefore, very suitable also as a city or an apartment dog. Sufficient daily exercise must, however, be assured.

Shoulder height 17–20.5 in. (44–52 cm) for males; 18–19.5 in. (47–49 cm) for females.
Hair coat: Dense, smooth, and waved, but not curly and fine like that of the other spaniel breeds.
Colors: White with orange or leather-color markings, or reddish and ticked. The nose is brown to dark pink with white spots.

Clumber Spaniel (Plate 1)

This is a sturdy spaniel breed, solid on lower legs, one of the British hunt spaniels that was bred with a line of French basset hounds. The Clumber Spaniel is of truly calm nature, a trait that is greatly appreciated by a hunter in a particularly richly game-stocked territory, as well as by owners who live in the city.
Height: 16–18.5 in. (42–45 cm).
Hair coat: Dense, silky, and smooth.
Color: Pure white with lemon-yellow or orange markings.

Cocker Spaniel, American (Plate 1) and Dutch Breeds

These two breed lines are derived from the English Cocker Spaniel; they differ mainly in size and body structure. The American type is smaller and appears distinctly different from the English because of the rounder skull and marked eyebrow line. Very dense, long hair grows typically on the legs and belly. This calls for more care and attention and for regular haircuts.
Height: No higher than 15.5 in. (39.5 cm) for males; no higher than 14.5 in. (36.5 cm) for females.
Hair coat: Head hair: short and fine; body hair: silky, smooth, softly waved. Full-feathered hair on the legs.
Tail: Not too short, and carried through from the line of the back.
Color: Solid black, red, or blond, but also with some white along chest and neck, or black and tan.

Outline of Pure Spaniel Breeds

Cocker Spaniel, English Breed

This type was originally bred in England for hunting lowland fowl and rabbits and is, today, the most widely known and numerous spaniel in Europe.

Hunters have become increasingly interested in this passionate swimmer and hunter, with the result that the dog is now a favorite companion for city dwellers too. This spaniel loves children and is affectionate and sensitive. *Caution!* His limitless appetite can easily lead to overweight.

Height: 15–16 in. (39–41 cm) for males; 15.5–16 in. (38–39.5 cm) for females.

Hair coat: medium-long, smooth, silky. Well-feathered legs.

Ears: Low-set, long-haired and silky.

Tail: Low-set root, not too short, with continuous line from back through tail.

Color: Solid black or red; also black with red marking (black and tan); also black and white; orange-white; black-white with tan; or orange-, brown-, or blue-ticked; or blue and tan.

Regular, continuous hair care is essential for these Cocker Spaniels, and stripping must be done frequently to avoid accumulation of matted, dense undercoat.

Field Spaniel

This dog is a breed developed from mixed blood lines of Cocker-Springer and Sussex Spaniels, and was specifically bred for lowland hunting. Like his relatives, this dog is also a very suitable house companion. His body appears long and sturdy because he is built on rather short legs.

Height: 17¾ in. (45 cm).

Hair coat: Not too short; silky and shiny; very lightly waved. Chest and belly hair slightly longer and curly.

Ears: Low-set, medium-long, nicely feathered.

Tail: Low-set tail root, trimmed to one-third length and carried slightly downward.

Color: Solid black, reddish gray, mahagony red-brown, golden-brown, or liver-brown.

English Springer Spaniel (Plate 2)

This spaniel runs on the highest land-spaniel legs and was used as a hunting dog as far back as the Middle Ages. His name stems from a behavioral pattern of fast forward jumping to retrieve the prey. This is an exceptionally fast dog with great endurance. He is just as well suited, however, to life with a family in a city.

Height: 20 in. (51 cm).

Hair coat: Dense and patted down, lightly wavy, weather-fit but not rough.

Ears: Medium long.

Color: White with black or liver-brown spots and flats, or with tan markings, but also all other accepted spaniel colors (except those specific for water and toy spaniels). The nose is black or brown.

Welsh Springer Spaniel (Starter)

This spaniel originated in Wales, stands a bit shorter than his English brother, and has the following other distinctions.

Height: 17 in. (43 cm).

Hair coat: Thick and silky; not too much wave.

Ears: Shorter than those of other spaniels.

Color: Full, dark red with white. The nose is dark or flesh colored.

Sussex Spaniel (Plate 1)

This spaniel was cross-bred from Clumber Spaniels and speed dogs and originated in the county of Sussex, England. He is the fastest hunting dog for searching in dense underwood thicket. Training this spaniel, however, is significantly harder than training the Clumber Spaniel. The Sussex Spaniel is very playful and loyal, but he is occasionally jealous of other dogs in the same household and spiteful toward them.

Height: 15–16½ in. (38–41 cm).

Hair coat: Richly waved with an emphasized collar.

Ears: Very long.

Tail: Cut to 5–7 in. length (13–18 cm).

Color: Liver-brown-gold with shiny golden hair tips. The nose is brown.

15

Spaniels

American Water Spaniel (Boylein Spaniel)

This is presumed to be a cross between the slightly larger breed of Irish Water Spaniels and the Curly-Coated Retriever. The dog is an excellent swimmer and retriever; however, he is not a pointer and only jumps the prey. He is suitable for fowl hunting and low brush work. Other characteristics are his excellent guard qualities and his good adaptability to families, as well as his affectionate and enterprising nature.

Height: 15–18 in. (38–45 cm).

Hair coat: Dense, curly, and soft; loosely curly-feathered at the legs.

Eyes: Dark brown or light brown.

Ears: Broad flaps, set just above the eyes; dense and curly and reaching down to the tip of the nose.

Tail: Moderately long, lightly curved, and carried slightly lower than the line of the backbone.

Color: Red or chocolate brown, occasionally with small white marks on the chest and toes.

Figure 4   *For specifics about hunting spaniels, you should consult a specialty breeders' club. Most hunting spaniels (French: epagneul) are cross breeds of spaniels, but they belong to different breed groups of hunting dogs.*

Irish Water Spaniel (Plate 1)

This spaniel is still of unknown derivation, although he has been bred for many generations. He is very enthusiastic about swimming and is a passionate fowl and feather hunter. Outside his home in England, this dog is well known and liked in the Scandinavian countries, whereas he is only rarely seen in continental Europe. The Irish Water Spaniel is also known as the clown of all spaniels; he resembles poodles a bit and is a well-liked, affectionate, and obedient companion.

Height: 20–23 in. (51–58 cm).

Hair coat: Tight, long curls, and thick bangs reaching down between the eyes.

Ears: Very long, close to the head, generously curled.

Tail: Partially curly only, almost hairless from about 10 cm downward.

Coat: Dark brownish red to rich, dark red.

Outline of Toy Spaniels

English Toy Spaniels

- King Charles Spaniel (after Charles I) (Plate 4)
- Prince Charles Spaniel
- Cavalier King Charles Spaniel (Plate 4)
- Ruby Spaniel
- Blenheim Spaniel

There are five distinct toy spaniel lines, all of which were derived in England by crossing small breeds with Japanese Chins, Pekingese, and the like. They have as common traits their relatively large round heads, heavily haired ears, silky soft, furry hair coats, and affectionate, tender, and sensitive nature.

Although toy spaniels were still used for hunting during the last century, they are, today, exclusively pet dogs. Their small size and undemanding nature make them suitable companions even in small living quarters.

Height: 10¼–12¾ in. (26–32 cm).

Outline of Pure Spaniel Breeds

Hair coat: Silky, long, only lightly waved.

Tail: Trimmed, with long feathered hair, and carried horizontally.

Color: The colors of the toy spaniels are their major distinctions:

- King Charles Spaniel: Shiny black with tan.
- Prince Charles Spaniel: Pearly white with deep black and red-brown markings. White forehead marking.
- Cavalier King Charles Spaniel: Solid, shiny, red, or pearly white background with markings in chestnut, black, or tan.
- Ruby Spaniel: Solid chestnut brown without any markings.
- Blenheim Spaniel: Pearly white with yellowish red or chestnut areas. Head with white forehead mark and, preferably, a red spot on the top of the head.

Papillon (French-Belgian Toy Spaniel) (Plate 4)

Bred in France and Belgium, this toy spaniel is compared to a butterfly because of his appearance. This dog has been bred since the thirteenth century and originally had a longer head. There are two types, one with standing ears and one with hanging ears. This spaniel is a good guardian and an undemanding companion.

Height: 8–11½ in. (20–28 cm).

Hair coat: Full and silky.

Color: Pearl white with variously colored spots and marks.

For more specific information about toy spaniels, you should get in touch with a registered toy spaniel breeder or kennel club.

Tibetan Spaniel (Plate 4)

While all other spaniels have the common trait of being instinctive hunting dogs, this spaniel has nothing of the sort. He is a very different line, comes from a far-away location, and has only his name in common with the other breeds of spaniels.

Tibetan monks bred these dogs originally, and trained them to move the prayer wheels. Later they became solely pet dogs. The breed developed from crosses between Lhasa Apso and Pekingese lines, and the Tibetan Spaniel has become a quiet, gentle, and affectionate dog that is well suited for city apartments.

Height: 9½–11 in. (24–28 cm).

Hair coat: Dense, closely grown hair with fine undercoat. Lionlike mane over neck and shoulders.

Ears: Highly feathered, hanging.

Tail: Carried curled over the back like a feathery plume.

Color: Solid black, gold, or light brown; but also black and tan, white, or cream colored.

The *Japan-Chin* and *Pekingese* breeds also belong to the Asian toy spaniel group. The international spaniel organizations can provide you with more detailed information.

Supplies and Housing for Your Spaniel

Before your new pet moves in with you, you had better visit a pet supply store. There you will find everything necessary for the care and grooming of your dog. Of course not everything offered is useful or even necessary.

Making products for dog owners to buy is a multimillion-dollar business, and it encourages many manufacturers to produce a variety of useless articles. To avoid overbuying, we suggest you follow the checklist of necessary supplies in this chapter.

Figure 5   *With an energetic and untamed puppy, it is best to use a learning harness to cope with the strong urge to pull ahead.*

Collar or Harness?

A harness is highly recommended for the spaniel puppy (Figure 5). At first you won't be able to prevent the dog from pulling ahead, even with a leash and collar, which can choke him.

We learned the hard way that the youthful exuberance of your young dog is better handled with the help of a harness; our first planned long walk with our cocker puppy startled us all. We had barely closed the garden gate behind us when our little Amigo fell down unconscious on our lawn. His collar had choked him while he was pulling forward, boisterous and happy about our upcoming walk together. But we learned from our mistake. Amigo was given a harness, and we had solved our problem.

If a harness is seen as detracting from the elegant appearance of this type of dog, a collar can be substituted when the animal has grown and been trained effectively.

Checklist of Necessary Supplies

- Harness, discussed above.
- Leash (standard length) to walk the dog.
- Long leash (you may be able to purchase one with an automatic roll-up device). This long leash serves for extensive walks as well as for obedience-training your puppy.
- A muzzle. This may be required in

Plate 3   *Stephan and his spaniel show their harmonious relationship.*

Plate 4   (above) *Cavalier King Charles*
Spaniel (left) and Papillon
(below) *King Charles Spaniel (Ruby)*
(left) and Tibetan Spaniel

rabies-endemic areas. You may also need one when taking your dog on a trip and perhaps for visiting the veterinarian.

- A sleeping box or basket large enough for the grown dog to stretch to his full length. Dogs like enclosed baskets, but the standard type can be kept cleaner more easily.
- A lining that keeps the dog warm but is not too soft. Any pet store can advise you. You may also use a blanket as long as you keep in mind that it must be laundered frequently.
- A food bowl. You need two bowls because cool, fresh drinking water must be available at all times. You can buy a specially shaped dish (smaller on top) for dogs with long ears, thus preventing those carefully groomed ears from dangling in the food bowl (see Figure 19). You may find useful a rack that accommodates two bowls and keeps them somewhat elevated, thus enabling the dog to eat and drink comfortably.
- A metal comb and a brush. If you let the pet-store owner know that you are buying the various supplies for a spaniel, he will be able to offer you the proper grooming articles for this type of dog. Comb and brush are all that are needed until your puppy's coat changes, after about the ninth month.

A Place to Sleep and a Place to Eat

Every dog needs permanent sleeping quarters with which no one will interfere. We have to take these needs into consideration, just as people do not readily give up their beds or favorite chairs. For the dog's quarters, choose a quiet place, free of drafts, and preferably in a location from which he can observe family activities (Figure 6). Spaniels dislike being alone, and, anyway, the dog has now become a permanent part of your family.

Always feed your spaniel in the same location; perhaps the most practical place is either the bathroom or the kitchen. Here the floor is usually cleaned easily, and there is no harm in an occasional spill on the tiles or linoleum.

Consider that dogs—even more so than we human beings—acquire certain habits. They possess an extraordinary awareness of time, and they suffer when confronted with frequent changes in their regular schedule. In this regard, a Cocker Spaniel can be a downright tyrant. Right from the beginning, plan his schedule on a permanent basis for the future.

Figure 6   *As sleeping quarters you should select a quiet place away from drafts.*

21

Ground Rules for Care and Maintenance

Dogs need a firm hand. They will always try to test the limits set for them and to go beyond them, if possible. If you vacillate and your behavior is inconsistent, your dog will quickly sense this and exploit your lack of decisiveness. Therefore, right from the beginning, remember this important principle:

Consistency is the key to a harmonious relationship between man and dog!

Adapting to the New Environment—The First Few Nights

Right from day 1, decide where the dog will have his permanent quarters and keep him there. If, in an initial burst of enthusiasm, you offer him the soft comforter on your bed, the dog will continue to try to settle there and you may find it difficult to keep him away.

The first night may well turn out to be extremely nerve-wrecking. Puppies behave just like babies—they cry when they are lonely. If you give in and pet or feed your spaniel, you will not get much sleep later on. The puppy will continue to blackmail you by whining and howling if he knows that this will cause his owner to come every time.

Give the dog the best of care, but do not give in to him in this way. He will soon get the message that he sleeps alone at night (Figure 7). You can make this transition easier for him by adding to his sleeping basket an object that carries your scent—an

old slipper, for example. Because the puppy has been used to sleeping nestled against the warmth of his mother's body, he needs some substitute during this transition period.

Figure 7   *Don't start this way! From the start the dog must know that this is* your *bed.*

Housebreaking the New Puppy

The puppy is still too young to know when and where to relieve himself. He will have to learn this, and it won't happen overnight. He has to learn how to control the urge to relieve himself by controlling his muscles.

22

Ground Rules

Be patient should your puppy have an "accident" inside your house. Let us not forget that puppies are like human babies; they have a right to gentle, sympathetic care. This includes tolerance in case of an accident during housebreaking. Neither slapping the dog nor dipping his nose into his excrements constitutes a suitable training method. Rather, say "No" in a voice that means business, and carry your puppy outside to the place you want him to use as a toilet.

A puppy needs to be taken out several times during the day—after feeding, drinking, and naps; when he awakens in the morning, or when he shows signs of sniffing the ground, turning in a circle (Figure 8).

As soon as you bring your puppy home, become aware of these signs and take him to his place outdoors, allowing sufficient time. Soon he will use the right place and will alert you of his needs. Praise the little chap each time he relieves himself in the proper place—at least six or seven times a day. In this way, the puppy learns that he did correctly what he was supposed to do. Furthermore, he will not want to forgo such warm praise in the future.

When going for a walk with your dog, do not allow him to relieve himself in the middle of the sidewalk. Right from the start, walk near the curb, allowing others to pass you without incurring their wrath, or else they may eventually direct their anger toward all dog owners. The annual license fee for your dog does not exempt you from consideration for your fellow men and women, for in the final analysis everyone is a taxpayer in one way or another.

Figure 8   *The dog's bathroom is always outdoors! Take the puppy to the same place from the start, and soon he will know where to go.*

Do Not Permit Your Dog to Beg

Included in providing the puppy with proper care is to train him not to beg. This may seem especially difficult for the snack-loving spaniel. You will train him as an exemplary companion and pet by being consistent at all times in this regard. Feed your dog before you have your own meals, and refrain from offering him morsels from the table.

Spaniels

General Rules for Grooming

If you have decided to get a spaniel, particularly a Cocker Spaniel with its shining, silky coat, you should know that it is a type of breed that requires grooming. Certainly beauty requires care, but cleanliness and good health also depend largely on regular grooming habits. Considerable effort and time are needed to keep a spaniel in good condition.

Hair Care

Until the dog sheds his hair at about the ninth month, do not use anything but a metal comb and brush. Use them often! After the ninth month, the dog needs to be brushed thoroughly about twice a week, at least. Do not wait until his hair is matted

Figure 9   *Only a well-groomed spaniel is a beautiful spaniel. Have the first typical spaniel haircut done by professionals.*

because grooming then becomes difficult and painful for both owner and pet.

Do not be tempted to use scissors to trim your dog's hair, especially if you are a novice. In order for the Cocker Spaniel to get the proper standardized haircut, we suggest you take him to an expert groomer—at least for the first few times, until you become more experienced (Figure 9). Your local spaniel kennel club will gladly supply you with any answers to specific questions you may have regarding correct hair care.

The Bath

Rarely will you be required to give your dog a bath. Never give your puppy a bath, and bathe a grown dog as seldom as possible, really only when the task has become unavoidable. Off and on, dogs want to smell a certain way, according to their own taste, achieved by rolling around in places which we as their owners consider distasteful (Figure 10). In such a case the smelly dog needs a bath. Never use scented soap; rather, get some specially formulated shampoo or dry shampoo at any pet store. After giving your dog a bath, dry him thoroughly and keep him away from any draft.

Keeping Eyes and Ears Clean

You will soon notice that small drops of mucus may collect in the corners of your dog's eyes, especially after sleeping. Wipe the eyes gently with a clean, lint-free cloth.

At least once a month, clean your dog's ears to prevent wax buildup. Use a cotton Q-tip dipped in warm water, and remove any wax carefully.

Ground Rules

Should you observe your dog frequently scratching behind his ears or vehemently shaking his head, consult a veterinarian. The dog may be suffering from an ear inflammation due to ear mites or from a similar ailment.

Figure 10 *Once your spaniel has taken a mud bath, you can only dry him with towels or (preferably) give him a full bath.*

Care of Teeth

Generally speaking, it is not necessary to brush your dog's teeth because they are cleaned in a natural way, provided of course that you do not feed him soft food exclusively. Dog biscuits, veal bones, or "bones" made from hide serve as the dog's toothbrush. If you notice tartar, gently wipe his teeth with cotton balls dipped into 3% peroxide solution. In severe cases, have the veterinarian remove the tartar in order to avoid inflammation and abscess of the root canal. These could eventually lead to loss of the dog's teeth and possibly to other problems.

Care of the Footpads

Check your dog's paws occasionally. Small pieces of stone or ice may become wedged between toes and footpads. Carelessly discarded chewing gum, for example, may stick to the paws' fine hair and create discomfort for your dog. Sprinkle some powder on sore footpads, and rub a dab of Vaseline on cracked surfaces. If you take your dog for a walk on a cold winter's day on salted roads, care for your pet's paws afterwards by washing and drying them and by applying either baby powder or Vaseline.

Ticks and Other Parasites

Ticks, which can become quite troublesome for dogs, may be dabbed with alcohol or oil and—after about 10 minutes—carefully removed with a pair of tweezers. Watch out that you do not leave part of the parasite's body in your dog's skin.

Rid your pet of other pests by using specially formulated powders, sprays, or soaps. Dust or massage his coat with them, according to directions, wait for the powder to become effective, and finally brush his coat thoroughly.

If you follow the above measures for care and grooming conscientiously and visit your veterinarian once a year for your pet's general check-up, you can consider yourself a responsible dog owner.

Spaniels

How to Treat Your Spaniel

Your Tone of Voice Is Important

When you are around your spaniel, the tone of your voice is much more important than what you say. The dog quickly learns to differentiate between your goodwill and your anger toward him. Moreover, small nuances between these two extremes, as well as joy and sadness, are soon perceived by your pet just by listening to your voice.

One instance in particular comes to mind. Children in our neighborhood called our cocker spaniel "Minko" or "Minkel." His real name, Amigo, must have sounded too foreign to them. We further modified the children's name by creating yet another nickname for him: "Minkel pinkel stinkel dog." Amigo was ecstatic everytime we called him that. He immediately ran for his bone or other favorite object and proudly strutted around the house, actions that in

Figure 12 *Puppies love objects that carry the scent of their master or mistress.*

his case were an expression of extreme happiness.

Of course, our dog did not attach any meaning to this nickname. However, he was able to recognize by the tone of our voice that we were joking with him, and that meant that we were in a playful and happy mood.

You can readily see that it is up to you to create a cheerful climate by consistently talking to your dog in a calm, friendly manner. Your pet will be all the more impressed when occasionally you feel that you must talk to him in a strict and firm voice (Figure 11).

Punishing

The best way to punish your puppy is to shake him, without lifting, by the scruff of his neck. Grab as much of the coat as you can, and shake as though it needs dusting. This is the way the puppy's mother behaves, although she uses her mouth. The result is the same: the puppy will recognize the physical superiority of his master or mistress, and this will leave a lasting impression on him.

Figure 11 *The tone of your voice alone can tell a puppy that he did something wrong.*

Ground Rules

Lifting Your Puppy

Never lift your puppy by the scruff of his neck. Instead, hold him with one hand around his chest and your other hand supporting his rump. This is the only way to carry him about safely and painlessly.

Playing—Suitable Toys

Nowadays dogs have been domesticated to such an extent that they have little chance to make use of their inborn instinct for hunting. Today we substitute playing with a pet dog for his inherent urge to hunt without displeasing the hunter. Also, we substitute play for flushing game; a spaniel will gladly chase a ball, for example. Taking a walk with your dog is important and enjoyable, but does not take the place of vigorous exercise that keeps those rarely used muscles in shape. For this reason you should make time to play with your dog on a daily basis. You can easily combine watching and playing with your dog. Of course, retrieving provides the greatest fun for your spaniel (Figure 13). However, be sure that any piece of wood, for example, that you throw for him to catch or fetch is strong enough to withstand his chewing or biting. Our dog Amigo got a splinter in his mouth in this way, and our veterinarian had to use an anesthetic to remove it.)

Your dog needs toys in your house or apartment as well. It does not matter what you give him (a ball, a piece of cloth, etc.), but be certain what his toys are made of. Certain commercially available squeezable dolls and some synthetic balls, which are too soft, can be a potential hazard to a dog that likes to chew on objects and may accidentally swallow bits and pieces.

Instead, allow your dog to play with safe and interesting toys, such as the formerly mentioned "bones" made of hide.

Suitable toys provide your spaniel with the opportunity to play by himself, and this can be of great help with a puppy—it lets him forget that there are rugs, carpets, and furniture on which he could chew!

Figure 13 *Retrieving objects gives your spaniel a chance to use his inborn hunting urges.*

Spaniels and Children

We mentioned elsewhere that the spaniel likes children, and would like to say a few words on how to maximize this interaction between child and dog. We suggest that three age categories be considered: babies, children up to 7 years old, and older children.

Spaniels

You will make a big mistake by entirely separating your baby from the dog. One cannot rule out the possibility that in this case your dog may fail to recognize the carefully protected infant as a family member. This may result in jealousy or, worse, a dog's desire for revenge. It is possible that a grown dog may try, in an unguarded moment, to get rid of the little "intruder" by biting him. Such incidents, frequently reported by the news media, can invariably be traced to the improper handling of dogs. Allow the dog and the baby to get used to each other by showing the infant to your dog and at the same time talking to him in a friendly voice. Perhaps your pet may want to sniff and smell your child, because the spaniel belongs to a type of animal that relies heavily on smell.

Figure 14 *Show your puppy the baby: this will make the dog understand that the newcomer is part of the family "pack."*

Please do not display an exaggerated fear of germs! If an animal has had all the prescribed shots, is free of worms, and is well groomed and cared for, there is no danger of his transmitting a disease to human beings. Furthermore, you need not hand over your dog to others during pregnancy because of the supposed danger of infections. However, about 6 weeks before the birth of the child, the veterinarian should check the dog for the possible presence of parasites or tapeworm.

Once your dog has sniffed and smelled the baby and has gotten to know the newcomer, he will readily accept the infant as part of the family and may even want to protect the little one. Do not give your pet grounds for jealousy. Try to show your love for both your child and your pet, and you will be rewarded with a satisfying, peaceful relationship among all members of your household.

Generally speaking, children under 7 years of age are not yet capable of handling a dog properly. They still lack insight into what may hurt the pet and what may feel good to him. Even a spaniel with the gentlest of dispositions will not allow someone to pull at his sensitive ears again and again, without retaliating (Figure 15). Smaller children also lack the physical strength necessary to hold the dog securely when he pulls at his leash. Under no circumstances should parents leave small children alone and unsupervised with their dog.

Children over 7 years of age, on the other hand, can make quite competent masters or mistresses for their dog, provided that they have grown up with him.

Ground Rules

Figure 15 *Spaniels love children. However, that love stops short of having their ears pulled!*

They have learned in a playful manner how to handle the animal properly. You can usually leave a 10-year-old child alone with a dog the size of a spaniel. One thing is certain: If you consider carefully, right from the start, all the points made above, your child and your dog may very well become the best of friends, each leaving his mark on the other.

Getting Used to Other Pets

Should you already own other pets, follow the same steps suggested for your baby: Introduce your puppy to all of them. Of course, when a grown dog is brought home as the new pet, you will want to proceed with more caution. If, after having made every conceivable effort to achieve a peaceful relationship, all have failed, do not hope that in time your pets may get used to each other. In particular, a relationship between a dog and a cat may create great problems. Some cats are entirely comfortable around dogs (either because they grew up with them or provided foster parenting), and others loathe dogs—and the same holds true for dogs.

By far the simplest situation is that of having a puppy get used to a kitten (Figure 16). It also takes just a short time for most dogs to get used to guinea-pigs and turtles.

A Second Dog

If you already own a dog and wish to add a companion for him, pay attention to the following: There will rarely arise any problems if the newcomer is still a puppy.

Figure 16 *Puppies and kittens that get to know each other early will usually become good friends.*

29

Spaniels

There may be problems, however, when two adult dogs are expected to get used to each other. For instance, we were the owners of a male Lhasa-Apso dog named Rusty when we acquired the 8-week-old puppy Amigo. The two got along famously. Of course the younger dog knew instinctively that he had to respect the rank and rights of the older dog and subordinate himself to the latter. This did not, however, affect Amigo's devotion and love for his friend, even later on, when Amigo eventually became the stronger and bigger of the two dogs.

If you already own an older female dog, we would advise you against getting another female. Not infrequently, these animals dislike each other enough to result in continuous fighting and problems. If you wish to have two bitches, it is better to start out with two littermates. Sister dogs usually get along well with each other.

When Your Dog Is in Heat

A female dog (bitch) will usually be in heat first between her 8th and 10th months of life, and this condition will last about 3–4 weeks. A male dog will be sexually mature around about 1 year of age and will then be able to mate at any time. On the contrary, a female dog is ready to mate for only a few days during the several weeks of heat. During this time, about 5 days, the bitch will accept mating, and the best chances for conception are considered to be between the 13th and the 19th days. Other important figures to remember are the following: at about 18 months of age, the bitch may first be mated, or more clearly stated, at the time of her second heat at the earliest; also, preferably, she should be first mated before she reaches 4 years of age, to avoid problems encountered at later first births.

Figure 17
If you take your bitch for a walk while she is in heat, you must expect ardent suitors. Caution! Even well-trained bitches will stray when they are in heat.

30

Ground Rules

After the mating has occurred, the two dogs stay joined for up to 15 minutes. The male organ of the dog reduces in size only slowly after the sperm has been introduced. It is, therefore, not only senseless but also dangerous to separate male and female dogs caught in unplanned mating. Both animals can incur serious injuries through forceful separation.

Canine gestation time lasts about 63 days. Add 2 months and 2 days to the date of the mating in order to calculate your dog's delivery date. Since not all births occur exactly as calculated, you must be prepared from the 59th day on.

Bitches can be in heat any time of the year, but spring and fall are more frequent. The specific scent of a bitch in heat can attract mature males from near and far, and sometimes there are whole packs of enterprising young males running after one female (Figure 17). They can manage most astonishing obstacles, such as fences, walls, and small openings. Their keen sense of smell will lead them with certainty to the house of a bitch in heat. Should the sought-out lady not be available because she is securely locked in, these unrelenting suitors will howl all sorts of wolfish songs to get attention.

To avoid pregnancy, there are three possibilities:

- Sterilization (removal of ovaries, uterus, or both).
- Hormone treatments, which should not be repeated because of possible complications.
- Protection of the bitch from male dogs. This is still the best method.

To save yourself and your bitch from howling suitors in front of your door, you should carry your dog for about 100 feet away from your house when you go for a walk. This procedure interrupts the scent track, and the male dogs will not be able to track the scent to your house. Admittedly, a spaniel is not a feather weight, but this burden is lighter than that of the uncounted howling lovers that must be dispersed, and that present a severe provocation to your neighbors.

While a bitch is in heat, even the most docile and obedient dog may tend to stray and fall victim to an unfortunate happening: accidental mating or, worse, a car accident! Bitches in heat MUST be on a leash!

If you plan to breed your spaniel bitch, you should become a member of a registered kennel club in order to obtain correct breeding information, registering requirements, and the necessary help in preparing for the delivery and the litter.

Birth of Pups

Preparations for the delivery must be made in advance. The place chosen for the birth and for the litter should be warm and quiet, away from drafts. An infrared lamp may be used if additional heat is necessary.

If you don't have a litterbox for the pups (you can buy one in a pet store or make it yourself), you can use thick layers of newsprint covered with some soft, clean rags or towels. The pregnant bitch should be familiar with the place about 2 weeks before the delivery date.

31

Spaniels

There are some signs that tell you the birth is close: the bitch is restless and refuses food; her breasts are swollen, and there are small droplets of milk on the teats; her body temperature is lowered to 98°F (37°C). The birth starts with slight labor pains, which increase and result in the fluid release after about 3–4 hours. Then the first pup will be born. Six, eight, or more puppies may follow, one every 15–30 minutes.

The mother will first free the puppy from its amniotic sac, then bite and sever the cord, and finally lick and massage the baby to stimulate breathing (Plate 6). Should this instinctive behavior of the mother not occur, a human helping hand must be ready to sever the cord, carefully rub the pup dry, clean the nostrils and throat of fluids, and place the newborn to the teat of the bitch.

To be prepared for unforeseen events, you should locate a veterinarian several days before the planned birth and note his or her phone number. If you are inexperienced with dogs or animal births, or if you are anxious, timid, or nervous about your dog's delivery, get in touch with a friend or neighbor who can stand by to offer experience and help. If you don't know anybody, call the kennel where you purchased your dog. Probably the owner will offer advice and aid. But let it be said again: Breeding spaniel dogs is not a game; rather it requires much responsibility, knowledge of genetics, time, effort, and, not the least, good luck. There is no shortage of dog breeders in general, and there is an abundance of knowledgeable spaniel breeders. In the interest of purebred dogs, spaniels in particular, let us not increase indiscriminate breeding and lower the still-excellent standards of these dogs. Poor breeding leads to weak, nervous, behaviorally disturbed animals.

A bitch does not have to have puppies to stay healthy! There are no health disadvantages to lack of pregnancy. One phenomenon that may occur with an unbred bitch is pseudopregnancy, that is, imaginary pregnancy. This looks just like a real pregnancy: about 8 weeks after the last heat cycle, the mammary glands enlarge and secrete milk. At this stage of pseudopregnancy a bitch can foster-feed orphan pups. If real puppies are not around, the "mother" will try to get hold of any number of toys and other objects, which she treats like a suckling infant. This condition calls for calm treatment and much understanding. If your animal is very nervous, you should get veterinary advice and medication.

Traveling with Your Spaniel

"I would rather tolerate some fatigue and a few inconveniences than be left behind by my owners." Every spaniel would tell you something along these lines if he could speak to you. He dislikes nothing more than to be left alone by his owners, especially for a period of several weeks. But no owner of a spaniel needs to forgo a well-deserved vacation or to hand over his pet to a kennel. Above all, a vacation becomes a matter of careful planning, as

Ground Rules

there are many hotels and motels nowadays that permit pets. Find out in advance, though; you may perhaps have to compromise with respect to choosing your vacation destination. Once you are well prepared and have selected a place not too far from home, which may even allow for enjoyable walks and hikes, then your vacation with your dog may well be pleasant and restful for all concerned.

Figure 18

Essentials for the Trip

● An international certificate documenting all necessary vaccinations and current health status, signed by your veterinarian. *Important:* The date of vaccination must preceed the start of your vacation by a minimum of 3–4 weeks, but not more than 12 months. When traveling to foreign countries, make sure to get all necessary vaccinations from your veterinarian for your dog, at least 4 weeks prior to your trip.

● If you are traveling by public conveyance (plane, train, bus, or ship), a suitable dog basket or other container for transport.

● Bowls for feeding and drinking.

● A basket or pad for sleeping.

● Leash and muzzle.

● Comb and brush, possibly some disinfectant.

● First-aid travel kit (your veterinarian will advise you on needed items).

● Canned or dry dogfood if the usual food to which your dog is accustomed is not available at your destination. Should canned or dry dogfood be new to your dog, get him used to it well before the start of your vacation, by slowly adding these new foods in small amounts to his regular meals.

Detailed information regarding regulations governing travel with your dog is available at the travel departments of the various automobile clubs and at consulates of the respective countries.

It goes without saying that your dog belongs in the back seat, when traveling by car. In order for your dog to relieve himself and to be able to move about for a while, short breaks when you are driving are essential.

Correct Nutrition for Spaniels

Homemade or Commercial Foods?

Even experienced breeders are divided on this subject. Some of them fervently reject commercial food, and feed their dogs mainly fresh meats such as muscle, heart, tripe, and liver; others swear by the reliable, consistent nutritional composition of canned and dry dogfood. There is, however, agreement about the need for supplemental foods such as boiled grains (rice, wheat, or oats) and fresh and lightly cooked vegetables. For an adult dog, you can mix one-third supplement with two-thirds ready food. Both feeding methods (homemade and commercial) can produce healthy, strong dogs, and most of the old prejudice against canned food has been proved wrong, most audibly so in the so-called dog paradise, England. Most important is the correct ratio of the food constituents necessary at any one age. Not every dog owner knows these proportions well enough to mix the correct components, and inexperienced dog owners are probably best served with high-quality store-bought food.

Another advantage of commercial food is that, whereas vitamins, for example, Vitamin B_1, are destroyed during cooking at home, commercial food preparation retains vitamins in correct amounts after short-term heating and sterilization. Also, the food is easily stored and keeps well without spoiling.

We visited a modern dogfood manufacturing plant and were impressed by the immaculate, stringent cleanliness that was enforced before, during, and after production. Modern scientific research within the same company guaranteed the correct proportions of vitamins, minerals, and other components known to constitute a carnivore's optimal diet.

Figure 19   *This is a practical food bowl that keeps the spaniel's long ears out of his food.*

Canned and dry dogfoods are offered in many flavors and consistencies. Many of the foods are complete and contain all necessary food elements.

Since dogs do not need carbohydrates in their food—they can readily metabolize them—there are two basic types of canned food: those that are meats and meat by-products only, and those that contain already mixed carbohydrates as grains or starches. It may be wise to add more rice or grain when a food-loving spaniel needs to go on a diet.

Correct Nutrition for Spaniels

Also, there are moist, semimoist, dry, and semidry foods, which are, basically, the same except that the percentages of moisture content are varied. A lack of moisture makes the food higher in energy equivalents, and fresh drinking water supplies the necessary fluid volume. Naturally, a dog on dry food will drink more water than one on a fresh meat and vegetable diet.

Despite all of the excellent commercial foods available, there are still some dogs, especially sick ones, that may not tolerate or accept these foods. In these instances you must consider the preparation of acceptable food. The following table gives guidelines for food preparation for normally developed and normally active dogs.

Food Plan for an Adult Spaniel

24–28 lb. body weight.
One meal per day with two small additional snacks; caloric requirement: 1000 cal. per day.
Total amount of food per day
When you feed commercial food:
1 can dog food + 3–7 oz. supplement = Plan 3
When you feed fresh meats:
1–1¼ lb. meat + 3–7 oz. supplement = Plan D
Caution! Do not feed cold or frozen foods. Thaw frozen food completely. Lightly cook all meats whenever possible.
Calcium and vitamin supplements should be taken according to the veterinarian's advice.

Food Plan with Weight and Caloric Measures

Age of Puppy	Weight (lb.)	Meals per Day	Daily Calories Needed	Canned Puppy Food				Fresh Meats Plan			
				Can Food	+ Supple-ment	=	Plan No.	Meat	+ Supple-ment	=	Plan No.
5–6 weeks	4–6	5	500–700	1	2 oz.	=	1	14 oz.	2 oz.		A
7–8 weeks	4–6	5	500–700	1	2 oz.	=	1	14 oz.	2 oz.		A
3 months	8–10	5–4	600–750	1½	4 oz.	=	2	20 oz.	3 oz.		B
4 months	10–11	4	1200	1¾	6 oz.	=	2	1½ lb.	5 oz.		B
5 months	15	4–3	1300	2	8 oz.	=	2	1¾ lb.	7 oz.		B
6 months	16–18	3	1300–1200	1¾	6 oz.	=	3	1½ lb.	5 oz.		C
8–12 months	18–20	2	1200–1100	1¾	4 oz.	=	3	1½ lb.	3 oz.		C

NOTE: Once you have chosen your favorite dogfood, you need only match the caloric contents indicated on the can or package with the required intake of your dog, as shown in the table for various ages and body weights.

Spaniels

Supplements to Commercial Foods
- Plan 1:
  Powdered milk or cottage cheese in small quantities. Oatmeal, simmered carrots, or cooked spinach. Mashed bananas. 1 egg yolk per week. As rewards: cartilagenous meat pieces, a little dry dogfood, a dog biscuit.
- Plan 2:
  Oatmeal or rice in one-half its volume of milk and one-half water. Cooked spinach, grated carrots, sliced lettuce, or half an apple. 1 tablespoon honey. 1–2 egg yolks per week. As rewards and for dental health: dog biscuits, bread crusts, cartilage.
- Plan 3
  Cooked rice, wheat, or grain cereal. Lightly cooked vegetables (NO beans, cabbage, or peas), parsley, grated carrots, or half an apple. 1 egg yolk per week. As rewards: veal bones, some dry food, a dog biscuit.

Menus for Fresh-Food Diets
A = Ground beef, minced veal, or cut-up chicken organ meats.

Oatmeal, powdered milk, or cottage cheese; occasionally some broth. Lightly cooked carrots or spinach, also raw carrots. Mashed bananas. Add some sunflower seed oil as fat supplement. As roughage and to give food more consistency, sprinkle uncooked cereal flakes over the food. 1 tablespoon cod-liver oil is advisable during winter. Rewards: as in Plan 1.

B = Minced veal, lean beef, or lightly boiled heart. Use the broth for mixing other foods. Oatmeal or rice with grated carrots, chopped lettuce, or half a grated apple. Uncooked cereal to thicken food or on top. Add a dash of salt. 1 tablespoon cod-liver oil in winter. From 10 weeks of age on, feed a calcium supplement. From the 12th week on, you may add some fructose or honey. Rewards: as in Plan 2.

C = Beef, heart, cartilagenous meats, tripe. Once per week some lightly cooked liver. All vegetables lightly cooked. Grated carrots or apple. 1 egg yolk per week. Milk diluted with water and a small amount of honey or fructose mixed daily in the food. Mineral supplement as in Plan B. Rewards: as in Plan 3.

D = Beef, heart, tripe, trachea, lung, liver. Cooked cereal, also uncooked; with carrots, spinach, or chopped lettuce or apple. Pinch of salt. Maximum 2–3 eggs per week. Mineral supplement is important to prevent deficiency disaster. To chew: hide "bones" or whole carrots. As rewards: veal bones (not after 5 years of age), some dry food, dog biscuits.

Proper Rations for Special Dogs

For Toy Breeds
For toy spaniels feed one half of the amounts given in the food plan table.

For Overweight Spaniels
Once overweight, the adult spaniel should fast 1 whole day per week. This will be healthful and should not worry you. If the dog still does not reduce on that schedule,

Correct Nutrition for Spaniels

Figure 20   *If you feed commercially prepared food, you can be quite sure that all nutritional needs are met.*

you must reduce the amount of food given on all other days, increase the dog's activities, or both.

For the Aged Dog

Quite naturally, the aged dog will reduce his food intake. It is preferable to feed more protein and to reduce the fats and carbohydrates. You may calculate roughly 10 percent less caloric intake.

With the above guidelines and knowledge of the age and weight of his or her dog, even a beginner should be able to raise and keep a healthy dog that's neither over nor underweight. Not all spaniels are alike in their requirements, and the amount of food must be adjusted to suit the particular dog.

Since spaniels differ not only in weight and age but also in metabolic rate, no exact amounts of food can be prescribed for all dogs. Hunting spaniels, which often have much more active lives, will obviously need more highly concentrated protein than house-bound spaniels. Generally, it can be said that you will easily assess your pet's food needs if you watch him regularly, weigh him sometimes, and quickly acquire an intuitive feeling for any adjustments, up or down, that are necessary for good looks and health.

Nutrition Tips

Don't feed your spaniel too hot or too cold foods. Keep foods at moderate temperatures. Do not allow food leftovers to stay around for long hours, as they may invite bacterial growth and spoil.

Bones: Dog Biscuits, Hide "Bones"

Soft veal bones or dog biscuits give a dog a chance to keep his jaw muscles in good condition. They also serve as excellent rewards, but must not be given too frequently in order not to upset the food plan. They are especially useful for young dogs in training. However, puppies should not get real bones, despite their great need to chew on anything while they are teething. A small amount of dry dogfood will serve better for puppies. "Bones" made from hides are also allowable for pups, and the young ones will not hurt their teeth or gums however much they may chew these "bones." You can buy them in supermarkets, pet stores, and many other outlets.

Your dog should always have access to fresh, clean drinking water in order to discourage his drinking from contaminated puddles and other polluted sources, which may cause infectious disease.

Dogs should rest right after feeding. It is therefore recommended that you walk your dog before feeding or not earlier than 1 hour after he has had his food.

Figure 21   *If you feed additionally from the table, don't be surprised if your dog becomes overweight.*

What to Watch for in Adult Spaniels

When your dog is grown up, his skeletal size remains constant, and so should his body weight. At that time, your dog will require only one meal per day. This is most easily managed if you feed him around noon, since that will leave enough time for

bowels and bladder to eliminate before night. To bridge the 24-hour gap from one meal to the next, you may give your spaniel two small snacks, as described in the food table (p. 35). However, be sure to include the snacks in the total calculated amount of food necessary for your dog's well being and good looks.

Be prepared for the fact that the adulthood of your dog may reveal itself by a sudden decrease in food consumption. Although this event may suggest illness or disease, you should not worry. Most spaniels will show this decrease in appetite without any other symptoms to worry about. However, should your dog refuse food for a prolonged period, or should lack of appetite be accompanied by diarrhea, constipation, or vomiting, you should seek a veterinarian's advice immediately.

A Weekly Fast—Yes or No?

Again and again one hears the statement that every dog should fast for one day every week, in keeping with his evolution from a wild hunting dog.

Well, there are, surely, some roly-poly, four-legged barrels that would be well served by a weekly fast! Also, in times of ill health associated with vomiting, diarrhea, or constipation, it is wise to reduce the food intake. However, all things being normal, there is no more need for a dog to fast weekly than there is for his master or mistress to do the same.

Let us remember: A dog stays not only healthy but also fit, slim, and active with regular food intake that is geared to his weight and age.

Raising and Training the Spaniel

It is widely accepted today, and has been proved by behavioral scientists, that dogs have evolved from ancient instinctive creatures into highly intelligent animals. Both soul and reason have been ascribed to dogs. We must take care with the definition and distinction of these ascribed attributes, as compared to their counterparts in human beings. However, crediting dogs in general with more than their ancient instinctive behavior, we must rank the clever, sensitive, and intelligent spaniel at the top of the list. You will agree if you have ever watched the expressive eyes of a Cocker Spaniel.

A spaniel will consider you a traitor should you break the dog-master bond by treating him unjustly—by his standards!

Your spaniel is prepared to accept a human being willingly as one of his pack—and at a higher rank. The foundation of this contract is built at the time you train the puppy, and it begins with the acceptance of his name.

Obedience Training

Obedience training is the most vitally important lesson you can provide for your dog. The thought of street traffic quickly brings to mind the fact that an untrained dog is easily caught under the wheels of a passing vehicle. But the wilderness also presents dangers for the untrained dog. If he runs away or, even worse, plays a track-and-chase game, he becomes a straying, poaching dog in danger of being shot by a forester.

No matter where you are, keep your dog on the leash until you are absolutely sure that he will obey your call or whistle. To achieve this obedience, you may find it useful to work with a long cord as a leash (Figure 22). Pull the cord slightly after each command, and have a reward ready for successful achievement. Repeat the same lesson over and over, even after you have discontinued the long leash.

Figure 22
Lesson with a long leash: Pull the leash lightly when you command "Come here." That way the puppy will quickly learn the meaning.

Spaniels

If, however, your dog still goes away for a long day of straying, but returns happily to your doorstep, do not lose your patience and do not punish the dog, since he is returning voluntarily—in his own judgment. It will confuse him if you punish him just when he is obeying the command "Come here"—late or not. Keep cool and praise the little rascal, no matter how hard it may be for you.

Punishment is effective only when you catch your dog while the mischief is being committed! Spaniels react very poorly to beatings, which often lead to biting and fearful behavior. Stern and consistent verbal admonishment is also more effective for spaniels than the commonly administered slap with a folded newspaper, which leaves most spaniels quite unimpressed.

The section "Punishing" (p. 26) will tell you more about desirable methods of punishment.

Generally, it can be said that the dog won't do what the pup hadn't been taught. Behavioral training starts on the day when the pup arrives in your house. At about 6 months of age a dog should be able to do the following:

- Obey commands such as "Come," "Sit," "Heel," "Lie down," "Out."
- Heel and walk without the aid of a leash.
- Behave calmly at home or in strange places such as public buildings, stores, or offices.
- Keep calm while traveling in a car, and not be tempted to jump out as soon as the door is opened, unless the command "Jump" has been given.

- Not beg for food or accept food from strangers.

It is very difficult, sometimes impossible, to teach a dog to do the above after he is much older than 6 months.

Obeying Commands

"Come," "Sit," "Place"

The first command "Come!," if disobeyed, should not tempt you to run after your little rascal, thus committing a major mistake and making him run even faster! Try the reverse—turn in the opposite direction! Your dog will hesitate to continue in the direction he has chosen. Continue firmly on your way, and in due time your little fugitive will follow you. Learn how to use this pack behavior of your dog, be generous with praise, have a small reward handy, and your lessons will soon be successful.

"Sit" and "Place" are the two commands most important for all dogs. To teach "Sit," hold the leash quite short so as to keep your dog's head up; then push down his rump while you give the command "Sit." There is not much he can do but sit down, and practice makes perfect.

For the command "Place" you press rump and neck down simultaneously until the dog lies down. Praise must follow immediately and consistently; otherwise the dog will lose his enthusiasm to learn more commands (Figure 23). Repeat these exercises at least two or three times each day. You will soon be successful.

Raising and Training the Spaniel

"Stand," "Out," "Heel"

The commands "Stay" and "Stand" are extremely important, especially when difficult or dangerous situations require that you put on the leash quickly. To teach your little pupil, you must keep the leash short, then say "Stand" while you pull the leash back and up, since you want to avoid having the dog sit down. Should he try to sit, you must lift his body by placing your supporting hand under his belly toward the groin, and lifting his hindquarters to standing position. Be generous with praise, and you will soon be rewarded by success.

The command "Out" or "No" should be taught for all those occasions where the dog should release an object or stop whatever he may be doing: stop running around, let

Figure 23 *Don't forget the reward after a successful command! Otherwise the student will lose interest.*

go of a ball or a dangerous bone, and the like. You must make sure that your dog does not resume his action shortly after obeying your command. In that case repeat the command in a firm voice.

"Heel" is an especially difficult command for the spaniel, which is a proverbial roamer. To teach this command, you must not use the harness that is otherwise recommended, since the dog must feel a harsh, short pull on the leash. For this lesson it is preferable to use a collar with a pull chain or a leather neckband that will contract when pulled.

Now, walk your dog on a short, loose leash, preferably along a quiet path with a wall or hedge on the dog's side (to avoid sideways escapes). The left side is preferred for this command. At the time you give the command "Heel," the dog's head should be approximately at the height of your left knee; that is the moment when you pull the leash strongly enough to get your pup's attention, since the little fellow is completely unaware of your intentions. You must not allow any forward pull during this lesson. A thin branch or stick is useful here; you can move it in front of the dog's nose every time he tries to surge forward. Remember not to use the stick to beat the dog, as this would defeat the purpose of your lesson.

All this you must repeat over and over, daily if possible. Start by walking slowly in order not to tempt your pupil to rush forward and pull. Should that happen anyway, it may be useful to give the command "Sit" and then start over with the lesson "Heel." Keep the leash short until

41

Spaniels

the dog fully understands the command. Only then, proceed to perfect the command using a long leash. Be careful not to be excessive in your demands and expectations. You must use much patience to be successful with even the most unruly spaniel pup.

Last, but not least, voice your commands firmly and clearly to be effective. Here is an example to the contrary. Our guest was a most gentle old lady who told us proudly about the training she had given her dachshund in accordance with the latest in obedience training literature. Meanwhile her dachshund was happily unaware of the gentle words she spoke, and her soft voice could not even command her dog back from the garden when she was ready to leave. There is no reason to shout or be angry at your dog, but you must learn to speak clearly and firmly and to be consistent in your demands.

Retrieving

Retrieving is in the very blood of a spaniel. However, a puppy enjoys running after a ball, shaking it ferociously—and then not returning it to his master or mistress. It takes much patience to teach him to return and release the "prey." Remember that the whole thing should remain a game.

Try to remove the ball easily and playfully at a moment when the pup is not holding on to it fiercely. Once you succeed, praise or reward the dog immediately and start over. Soon the dog will love the game and even prod you to play more than you would opt for.

Here is an example of the value of your dog's training. We were very proud that our Cocker Spaniel Amigo would stay sitting any place until we relieved him with the command "Come here." Every day we increased the distance a few feet between the sitting, waiting dog and us before we called him to come. One evening he waited for his command, and when he arrived, he placed my key case at my feet. I had lost it at the last place of command, and I would never have been able to find my keys in the high grass if I had not noticed the loss until later in the walk. Luckily Amigo had learned to retrieve—and he deserved his special reward.

Figure 24

A few more hints may be helpful. Use the innate playfulness of your dog for his training lessons by leading from games into commands or tricks. Be sure not to ask too much of your pupil too soon in order not to discourage him. Praise generously, punish sparingly, and never beat the dog. Only a happy dog will be a successful pupil!

Raising and Training the Spaniel

Since you do not intend to make your dog a slave or to train him for circus acts, you must rely on patience, love, and persistence to turn your spaniel into a reliable, happy companion. There are special books on the subject of dog behavior that deal in depth with many aspects of this chapter. A small book such as this can cover only the basic points.

Figure 25 *Spaniels are excellent swimmers. They love to retrieve a ball from water.*

Training for the Hunt

Let us consider the training for daily-use commands to be the "primary school education" of your spaniel. There is, beyond that, the training for specific uses of the spaniel, which we can consider the "secondary school training" or the "vocational school or advanced training." There are two majors for which spaniels, specifically Cocker and Springer Spaniels, qualify: one major leads to graduation as a drug-sniffing specialist; the other, to the more significant specialty of hunting. The latter is the more genetically suitable and inherited vocational ability common to most spaniel types. Unfortunately, the professional sporting spaniel has become scarce as more and more of the breed are being kept as house companions. With this development the public is naturally more inclined to be interested in problems and questions relating to the spaniel as a family member rather than in those related to his role as a hunter. However, we will not completely neglect the hunting spaniel here.

The sporting student spaniel will have to attend classes devoted to sniffing, searching for, finding, retrieving, and delivering prey. One of the most difficult "courses" in this teaching plan is that which deals with the natural instinct of the spaniel to devour the prey he has caught. This instinctive behavioral urge must be changed into the retrieving pattern. The dog has to become a reliable retriever in order to be a useful member of the hunting team. Dog and hunter must trust each other equally.

Before serious training is begun, you should participate in the testing meetings that are arranged in various geographical areas by the spaniel kennels. A dog that is considered for hunt training must fulfill certain requirements in regard to sniffing, ability, willingness to search and flush, innate capabilities as a hunter, enjoyment of water (Figure 25), ease of leading and being led, reaction to shotgun noise,

Plate 5   *Tricolor male Cocker Spaniel.*

retrieving capabilities, and the like. It is quite fortunate that an increasing number of spaniel owners attend these tests and plan the training of their spaniels even without the prospect of future hunts. More and more people recognize and appreciate the fact that all of the lessons learned can be applied to many types of life styles.

Every specialist in the field of dog training knows how voluminous, intensive, and complex is the lesson plan for sporting dogs. This type of training should therefore be left to professional trainers and carried out under the careful eyes of experienced hunters.

Figure 26 *The high point of spaniel training is the training for the hunt.*

When Your Spaniel Is Sick

Before we discuss some of the symptoms of disease, let us take a brief look at the anatomy of the dog.

A Short Lesson in Dog Anatomy

The skeleton of the dog consists of 256 fixed or articulated single bones. The shoulder blades underlie the point of the back that is used to measure the "shoulder height" of the dog (floor to highest point above the shoulder blades). The thoracic and sacral vertebral column is so situated that it allows the dog to lie down curled up and also to move his hindlegs far toward and under the front when he is running fast. Jumping and adaptable types of walking are made possible by the special tarsal and metatarsal joints of the hindlegs, which consist of many small, articulated bones that enable the foot to adapt to various types of surfaces and strains.

The many (about 250) varied muscles of the dog are built and nourished by the protein, carbohydrates, and fats in his food. Most of the energy derived from food, however, is turned into heat, which is vital to keep the body temperature constant.

Heart and lungs are especially strong in the dog. These organs give these animals their unusual endurance and speed. The

Plate 6   *Spaniel puppies are born.*
(above) The bitch breaks the water bag (left) and dries the newborn by licking it vigorously.
(below) The new pups have their first meal.

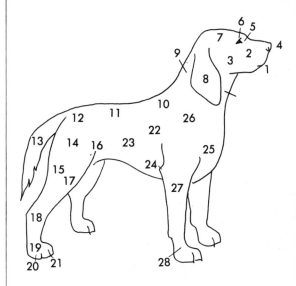

1. Lips
2. Muzzle
3. Cheek
4. Nose and Nostrils
5. Stop
6. Eyes
7. Skull
8. Ears
9. Neck
10. Withers
11. Back
12. Rump
13. Tail
14. Hip
15. Thigh
16. Flank
17. Knee Joint
18. Hock
19. Foot
20. Toes
21. Claws
22. Ribs
23. Abdomen
24. Elbow
25. Chest
26. Shoulder
27. Forearm
28. Pastern
29. Throat

Figure 27   *The parts of a dog's body.*

Spaniels

stomach can accommodate a single large meal; and the urinary bladder can store large quantities of urine, thereby enabling the male dogs to mark out large tracts of territorial ownership. For dogs the most significant external organ is their innervated, sensitive nose with its keen olfactory capability. The nose is, in a sense, the dog's compass. Figure 27 shows the locations and names of the various parts of the dog's body.

Health Problems—Diseases and Their Signs

There is only one type of good health, but there are many types of ill health and disease. When we do not feel good, we are conscious of our pains and ailments and can communicate them to others. Dogs, however, cannot tell us exactly what is wrong. We must therefore know and observe our dogs very closely in order to detect changes in their behavior early in the development of disease. Does the dog, for example, eat more or not at all? Does the puppy suddenly drink excessively? Is the usually exuberant chap lazy or lethargic, irritable, or sensitive to your touch? All these signs may be indications of ill health. Certainly you know that there is something wrong with your spaniel when his usually shiny hair coat turns dull and, maybe, his eyes have lost their normal sparkle.

Some dog owners will try at first to experiment with cures for their dogs. Do not attempt to do so, as you may do more damage than good and prolong the illness.

A sick dog must be seen by a veterinarian (Figure 28), preferably each time by the same one. A doctor who has seen and knows his or her patient from previous visits can diagnose disease more easily, faster, and more accurately. You can and must help the veterinarian by enumerating even minor changes in behavior and appearance.

If, however, you cannot reach a veterinarian immediately, you must be prepared to act provisionally on your own. For this situation each dog owner must learn some basic facts about first aid and be prepared with essential remedies and supplies.

Figure 28 *If your spaniel appears seriously ill, don't experiment; take him to a veterinarian immediately.*

48

When Your Spaniel Is Sick

The condition of the hair coat is a reliable criterion. Changes signal health problems reliably.

Lackluster hair may be caused by inadequate or incorrect food, vitamin or mineral deficiencies, or hormonal imbalance. Dull hair can also be a consequence of worm infestation or of lingering infectious disease.

Hair loss can have a multitude of causes, such as parasites, fungal infections, hormonal imbalance, eczema, and allergies. Advanced age may also be a reason for hair loss; so are kidney problems, poisoning, and many other agents.

When your dog's *hair stands up on end,* this may not be due to anger; skin abscesses, allergies, and impacted pores can cause the same symptom.

A *dry, warm nose* is not necessarily a sign of disease, although the normal nose feels moist and cool. In case of doubt, take your spaniel's body temperature.

Continuous nose licking may be caused by a nose cold or by a foreign body in the tongue or nose, as well as by a sore throat.

Sneezing and *coughing* can be due to respiratory disease, tonsillitis, or a foreign body in the throat area. Should the temperature be higher than normal, you must consider distemper, too. Old dogs may be plagued by chronic cough and may need to have their hearts checked. A veterinarian will prescribe appropriate medicine.

Pale mucosal surfaces around the eyes and the gums may indicate loss of blood or possibly poisoning.

Tearing eyes may be caused by catarrhal conjunctivitis due to draft or infection.

Don't bother with boric acid! Instead, use a clean, lintfree cotton cloth to remove the discharge, thus reducing the local irritation. If fever is also present, you must think of distemper as a possible cause.

In all of these cases you should consult your veterinarian for the diagnosis of the causative agent.

A head continuously inclined to one side is frequently a sign of external or internal ear trouble or, in the worse case, of a brain disease. Remember that a dog is sensitive to sound frequencies inaudible to human beings, and these may cause him to tilt his head in intensified concentration.

Shaking the head is usually a sign of a foreign body in or around the ear, but you must also consider the possibility of an internal inflammation of the ear.

Figure 29

49

Spaniels

"Skating" or *gliding on the rump,* especially on the carpet, is usually the result of itching around the anus. This may be caused by a slight injury, a small foreign body, an inflammation of the anal glands, or chronic worm infestation. If you cannot find the causative agent, you must get treatment by a veterinarian.

Frequent scratching may be caused by external parasites, such as lice, fleas, or ticks. You can treat these with baths, powders, or sprays. Such supplies are available in the pet departments of supermarkets and department stores and in pet stores. Scratching can also be due to allergies, to hormonal imbalance, and, if habitual, to boredom. Whatever the cause, scratching should be diagnosed and treated.

Swelling of the mouth, gums, tongue, or face is usually caused by an insect bite, often a bee sting. In normal cases the swelling will soon reduce despite its initially dangerous appearance. Should the swelling affect the tongue, however, you must watch out that breathing is not impaired.

Fever is most frequently a sign of generalized disease, mainly an infectious disease. Consult a veterinarian. Indications of fever are dull hair and eyes, lethargy, and increased warmth at the touch. Fever is a natural reaction of the body to fight an insult to one or more of the physiologic systems. If the temperature passes 102°F, you should consider a general and more serious disease.

Vomiting is not necessarily a sign of disease: when a dog devours his food too fast or eats too much, he will frequently then eat some type of grass in order to vomit and thus relieve his overloaded stomach. Of course, a dog may also vomit because of car or train sickness. You can prevent or alleviate this by giving him an anti-motion-sickness pill before the trip. Should vomiting recur repeatedly or be accompanied by elevated temperature, the cause may be a serious illness of the intestines, poisoning, or distemper.

Diarrhea can have many causes. An uncomplicated case of diarrhea without fever may respond favorably to some mint tea with a pinch of salt. Fluid replacement is important to make up for the fluid loss due to the diarrhea. Remove solid food for 1 day, and in most cases you will soon see an improvement. After the first day of fast you should feed your dog some oatmeal with finely grated apple, and you can add 1 or 2 charcoal tablets. If your dog refuses this diet, you may add just a bit of chopped beef to enhance the flavor. Our Cocker Spaniel Amigo had a favorite remedy for a sick day: a shot glass of brandy mixed with an egg yolk!

Diarrhea that persists for 3 days without significant improvement must be treated by the veterinarian, especially if fever becomes part of the syndrome.

Excessive drinking can be caused by high salt content in the diet. Drinking may also be increased with fever and during or after diarrhea. Continued excessive drinking, however, may be a sign of diabetes, kidney disease, or (in the bitch) uterine disease.

Dark urine may be caused by food components, but it may also be a sign of abnormal kidney or bladder function.

Blood in the urine is always a warning

When Your Spaniel Is Sick

signal, usually of a serious cause, commonly a kidney or urinary tract problem. Get veterinary attention immediately.

Blood in the stool also must always be taken seriously. Coupled with vomiting, it may be caused by poisoning. This may be life threatening, and the dog should immediately be taken to a veterinarian.

In regard to *intestinal parasites,* the puppy should be wormed before you purchase him. All puppies must be considered to have worms, and all should be treated accordingly. The veterinarian will prescribe the correct medicine and the schedule for repeated treatment. Older dogs are not as frequently plagued by worms as young dogs are; however, when diarrhea persists, the stool should be examined for parasitic eggs or worms.

Cramps may be the consequence of a generalized infection, an acute metabolic imbalance, poisoning, or other abnormal condition. Muscle cramps, however, are not uncommonly due to excitement or excessive irritability.

Limping is most frequently found in aged dogs and is usually caused by arthritic problems. In rare cases limping may accompany weakness, distemper (p. 52), or leptospirosis (p. 52).

Eczema can arise on any part of the body surface. It usually starts as an itching spot, which becomes infected because the dog scratches and breaks the skin. Some spaniels have a tendency toward eczema on the lower lips, which shows as moist, poorly healing lip sores. This disorder must be treated with a medicine prescribed by your veterinarian. It is important that you clean the area carefully each time you apply the medication. Since the location is associated with the fold of the lower inside lip, there is a tendency for spoiled food remnants to collect on the sore. The wound area must be very clean before the topical medication is applied.

Tumors may be benign or malignant. The size, location, and speed of growth are not related to the seriousness of the tumor. It is therefore important that you consult your veterinarian, who may need to take a biopsy specimen to diagnose the type of tumor. Benign tumors can be removed, if good appearance or movement require removal. Malignant growths can be treated, and many cured, in as varied ways as modern medicine knows.

Pseudopregnancy (imagined pregnancy) is a behavioral disturbance caused by hormonal functions (see also p. 32). This problem is most frequently seen about 8–9 weeks after a bitch was in heat without conceiving. The mammary glands start to enlarge, and milk production sets in. You can help alleviate the problem by increasing your dog's activities, reducing the protein content of the food, and avoiding excessive drinking. The enlarged and often warm breasts can be treated several times a day with cold water compresses on which you may sprinkle some vinegar. Several camphor rubs are also recommended. If you cannot achieve reduction of the symptoms within 10 days, ask your veterinarian for hormonal treatment for your bitch.

Spaniels

Common Serious Infectious Diseases

Every dog owner—especially the owner of a young dog or puppy—must know the most frequent and serious infectious diseases of dogs and the symptoms by which to recognize them. At the time you get your dog, you must make sure that all regular immunizations have been given. If you check these basic preventive measures carefully, you can be quite sure that your dog will be safe from the most common dog diseases.

Distemper
Symptoms: Fever, diarrhea, coughing, tearing eyes.
Advanced stages: Motion disturbance, cramping, convulsing.
This is a dreadful disease with very little chance of recovery. It affects young dogs most seriously, but older dogs also frequently are left with disturbances of the central nervous system.

This viral disease is effectively prevented by immunization before the 8th week of life, with a booster shot 4 weeks later, then follow-up boosters every 2–3 years.

Viral Hepatitis
Symptoms: Fever, inflammation of the nasal and throat passages, diarrhea, sensitivity in the belly region.
Like distemper, this viral disease destroys more young dogs but can attack dogs of any age. Survivors often are left with complications such as keratitis and blindness. Afflicted dogs must be treated immediately with serum, antibiotics, and special vascular support fluids.
Immunization is very effective and should be given at the same time as distemper shots.

Combination vaccines available today provide a practical way to have your dog vaccinated against several diseases at the same time and have him also receive the various booster shots at the same intervals.

Leptospirosis
Symptoms: Fever, lethargy, anorexia (loss of appetite), vomiting, weakness in the hindlegs, tonsillitis, stomach, intestinal, and kidney problems.
Advanced stages: Jaundice, motion disturbances, foul mouth odors.
This is a bacterial disease, must be treated immediately, and is best prevented by vaccinations given at the same time as the vaccines mentioned above.

Rabies
Symptoms: Abnormal behavior, biting without provocation, paralysis, convulsions, weight loss, hostility, aggression.
This is a deadly, incurable disease, and must be reported immediately to the health department.

The causative agent is a virus that is most frequently transmitted by the saliva of the affected animal. A suspected animal must be quickly taken to a veterinarian and kept under quarantine. Persons who have had contact with a rabies-suspect dog should consider receiving preventive immune serum.

When Your Spaniel Is Sick

Puppies can be immunized from 6 weeks of age on. Most modern vaccines are good for 3 years. All vaccinations will be recorded in writing by your veterinarian. Keep these records.

The description of these four major diseases that threaten a dog's life should not disturb you but rather impress on you the urgency for conscientious followup with the vaccination schedules of your new puppy or older dog.

The available vaccines are effective, relatively inexpensive, and combined for ease of record keeping. There are hardly any side effects to worry about, and the vaccinations do not affect you as owner at all (except financially!).

These vaccinations are valid internationally. For that reason you must keep your records, especially if you should plan a trip to a foreign country or even travel to hotels or other lodgings where proof of immunizations would be required. Also, dog kennels and dog hotels will require these papers, as well as your local licensing office.

Viral Diarrhea (Parvo- and Corona-Virus Diseases)
   Symptoms: Diarrhea, bloody (reddish or red) diarrhea.
Two types of viral diarrhea, caused by parvo and corona viruses, have taken an increasing toll of puppies and young dogs. A specific immunization is not yet available, but your awareness of the diseases will ensure that your dog has veterinary care in the earliest stages and thereby may save his life. With the slightest red discoloration of the stool, you should rush your dog to the veterinary clinic and obtain supportive treatment and testing for the causative agent. A preliminary parvo-virus vaccine may then be recommended.

Handling and Restraining Your Spaniel

You cannot help your dog achieve and maintain good health unless you learn some basic dog-owner's know-how.

Taking the Dog's Temperature
   Insert a rectal thermometer with some Vaseline or a similar lubricant into the anus. Leave the thermometer in place for about 3 minutes. This procedure is done most easily with two persons, one to hold the dog firmly around the chest and lift the tail at the same time, and the other to handle the thermometer. Remember that you should talk quietly to your dog to comfort him.
   A temperature above 102°F should be considered a fever.

Weighing Your Dog
   This is most simply done by picking your dog up in your arms and weighing yourself and the dog (Figure 30). Then weigh yourself alone, and subtract your weight. A normal adult Cocker Spaniel weighs 24–29 pounds.

53

Figure 30 *Which one of us gained the weight?*

Medicating Your Spaniel

Pills or powders are most conveniently given inside little balls of chopped meat or other favorite treats. Be sure to watch the whole thing being swallowed, and help it along by placing the ball as far into the mouth as possible.

Drops and other fluids are most easily applied by pulling the lower side of the lip slightly away and causing it to make a sort of pocket. By lifting the head of the dog slightly and applying the fluid carefully inside the lip pocket, you will force the dog to lick and swallow the medication. If you hold the dog's mouth and nose closed, there is little choice but to swallow.

Suppositories are usually best applied by two handlers, although this depends on the nature of your relationship with your dog and his inborn and acquired temper. One person should hold the dog and talk calmingly, while the other inserts the suppository carefully as far as possible into the rectum.

Holding and Restraining Your Dog

For many types of care the dog must be restrained. It is safest to place your arm around the body of your dog so that his head rests in the nook of your elbow. This leaves your other hand free to pet him, to apply firmer restraint, or to give medication. If the dog is in a biting temper or in shock, you will be better off to place a muzzle over his mouth. If you don't have a muzzle, you can tie a sling around the mouth, and then tie the cloth under the lower jaw and again behind the head.

First Aid

This requires calm action and clear thought. First you must try to calm the injured animal by speaking reassuringly and petting him if he does not resist your touch. The next step is immediate transfer to the veterinary clinic. If the dog is seriously injured, it is recommended to phone the veterinarian ahead so that the clinic is prepared for a specific support treatment.

Superficial wounds can be protected temporarily by placing clean bandages or clean cloths on them. To avoid additional irritation and inflammation, do not use any powders or ointments.

When Your Spaniel Is Sick

Internal injuries or loss of consciousness must receive immediate attention from the veterinarian. Do not try to instill fluids!

Contusions or *bruises* are best treated with cold compresses in order to reduce swelling.

If the dog has taken *poison,* it is best to find out which type was taken and then call the local poison control center or your veterinarian, before you instill water or cause your dog to vomit. Depending on the type of poison, either may be right or wrong, and the wrong guess can cost the dog his life.

Bleeding may be stopped by applying pressure on the open wound or, if the injury is major, by placing a tourniquet above the bleeding wound. The tourniquet (bandage, string, fabric) must be placed tightly enough to stop the bleeding. It should be released every 30–60 minutes. Take the shortest route to the closest veterinary clinic.

The Dog's Medicine Cabinet

Every spaniel household must have for the dog a specific medicine cabinet or an equivalent space, out of children's reach and supplied with medicine, ointment, powders, bandages, scissors, tweezers, and the like.

Caution! Outdated and unlabeled medications belong in the trash!

Transport to the Veterinarian or Animal Hospital

A large, strong carton, lined with the dog's or another familiar blanket, serves as a suitable bed for the transport of a sick animal. For a toy spaniel you may prefer a small carrying bag or an ordinary shopping bag with handles.

To lift the animal, place one arm around the middle of the hindlegs and support the dog's chest with the other arm.

Seriously injured or unconscious dogs may need the help of two persons to be carefully placed sideways on, or into, a container for transport. If the dog is unconscious, you should pull his tongue to the side of the mouth in order to prevent him from choking.

Caution! Shock and pain may cause the calmest and gentlest of creatures to bite suddenly!

Humane Euthanasia

A dog should be put to sleep only when extreme injury, incurable disease, incessant pain, or other such extenuating circumstances reduce the quality of life below humane standards.

A desire to get rid of a healthy dog is not an acceptable reason to kill him. Old age alone is not sufficient cause either. Dogs can function quite well without one or the other sensory organs, and loss of sight or sound is not reason enough to end their lives.

Spaniels

When the decision cannot be avoided, however, and all alternatives have been considered and found unacceptable, the necessity to kill the animal humanely must be faced. We had to make this traumatic decision when our spaniel Amigo suffered from incurable plant poisoning. After all methods of saving the dog had been exhausted, the veterinarian gave him an injection, just like administering anesthesia. Amigo sat in his master's lap and fell asleep painlessly, as if he were taking one of his favorite snoozes. The pain for us remained, mitigated only by the thought that we were able to spare Amigo weeks or months of an excruciatingly slow and painful death.

Understanding Spaniels

Short History of the Breed

Most spaniel breeds are derived from British retriever dogs. The best known and most widely found breed is the Cocker Spaniel. The name is probably derived from "woodcock" or from "cock pheasant," prey animals that had to be sought and retrieved during hunting expeditions. The family name "spaniel" is of more questionable background, suggesting a derivation from the name of the country Spain or (more likely) from the Carthagean word *Span,* meaning "rabbit."

It also remains unknown whether spaniel-type hunting dogs came long ago from the Middle East to Western Europe. Regardless of that possibility, spaniel dogs are today accepted as being of British origin. Some facts and figures are of interest: Spaniels have been on written record since 948 in certain law texts, as well as in 1594 in Shakespeare's *A Midsummer Night's Dream.* As of 1893, the Cocker Spaniel was registered as a specific breed, and since 1907 spaniel hunting-dog kennels have existed in Germany and other countries.

The father of all pet dogs is the wolf. There are, today, about 300 breeds of domestic dogs. Domestication of the dog can be traced back for 12,000 years. Despite this extraordinarily long time of adaptation to human lives, dogs still retain many types of wolf behavior. Wild dogs still live in packs as wolves do. Domesticated dogs consider the human family they live with as part of their pack. Their pack leader is their owner or master/mistress, to whom they are subordinate and whom they obey and follow. Dogs' hunting instincts are also a remainder from their wolf background.

Behavioral Characteristics of Dogs

The behavioral patterns of dogs are a result of several combined influences, such as domestication, original instincts, specific environments, and particular human indoctrination. You can therefore assume that a dog is more wolfish in nature the less contact he has with people. With increasing human contacts, the dog adapts accordingly to human patterns and accepts his master or mistress as leader.

Despite the wide variety of individual learning abilities among dog breeds and single dogs, there are overall generalized behavioral patterns and abilities that we consider basic dog behavior. They all use similar modes of expression by way of body and voice language.

Vocal Communication

A dog's way of speaking is generally called barking. It includes a broad scale of sounds, from a high-pitched whining to true barking, howling, or snarling, and many intermediate sounds as well. The dog can therefore use a very specific sound or sound combinations for specific occasions, and those who are willing to listen carefully will soon understand the different meanings.

Spaniels

Body Language

Much of this mode of expression is carried out with the tail. A wagging tail is friendly language; a tail tucked under denotes fear or guilt. Dogs with stumpy tails like the Cocker Spaniel, of course, find it harder to tell their story. They usually use their whole rumps to express joyful emotion!

Naturally, you must observe the overall body posture as part of their body language. Your spaniel is not always dog-tired when he lies sprawled out on the floor. This posture may just express a relaxed, contented mood. In such cases Amigo favored lying with his head slightly raised, on a pillow or an armrest.

When the dog's body is stretched out tensely, there are two reactions to watch out for. One is friendly and joyful and is expressed by tense concentration combined with a happily rotating tail. The other reaction shows tenseness accompanied by the neck hair standing on end; this must be considered an expression of anger, a warning step before defense or attack.

Gestures and Facial Expressions

To understand dogs better, we must also consider their gestures. Their facial expressions will frequently tell you their feelings. The typical Cocker Spaniel melancholic face is, certainly, not the only one these dogs can present. Their faces are just as apt to express joy, anger, stealth, contempt, or disappointment—if you are willing to observe them closely.

Of course, your spaniels cannot point their ears, since they are pendulous.

However, these ears, despite their weight, can be lifted to a certain angle when the spaniel is listening in a concentrated fashion. This looks rather cute but is not appreciated by show-dog judges, who are looking for low-set ear flaps.

Mouth, lips, and tongue are, equally, gesticulating instruments. There is a certain type of dog smile that some dogs are capable of by pulling the corners of their lips way back and baring their teeth at the same time. The tongue, also, is frequently used as a tool to express friendly feelings, tenderness, and love. Regardless of our human dislike for the licking habit, we must not forget that this behavior is a natural, loving means of expression.

It is fairly easy to teach a dog to shake hands—or paws, and this gesture is used, also, to beg for something. It is a natural one since birth, when the puppy uses his little paws to stimulate the milk flow in his mother's breasts. Lifting a paw to shake hands with a human being is a natural progression from this puppy behavior.

Burying Bones

Wolfish behavior requires storage of food for times of need. The domestic dog has retained this behavioral pattern and tries to dig holes to bury bones and food scraps, despite a usually plentiful food supply. Some dogs will not only try to follow this ancient urge in the garden, but will also attempt to bury items under the carpet, in a dark corner, or under a piece of furniture. Reflexive scratches even on hard surfaces are evidence of how firmly ingrained such ancient genetic traits are.

Understanding Spaniels

Amigo was a typical example in this respect and subjected us to an amusing—but embarassing—experience. We expected dinner guests, and the house reflected the delicious scents from the kitchen, except in the dining room, where

Figure 31   *Dogs will habitually bury bones and other food scraps under the carpet, potted or outdoor plants, cupboards, and so on. This is a residue from their wolfish background.*

the festive table was set but a bad odor of unknown origin was detectable. We suspected a hidden food treasure of Amigo's but could find nothing by the time the guests arrived. The evening went well despite my observation that one couple commented to each other on the peculiar odor.

Amigo, the culprit, personally solved the mystery the next evening when we sat back to watch television. He got up, walked over to our giant philodendron tub, and unearthed a foul-smelling bone (Figure 31)! As far as he was concerned, his meal was long past—and here was his stored food, just in time for an evening of dearth. The poor "starving" creature had proudly put his forebears' instincts to work.

Circling

Circling several times in the spot where a dog is about to curl up and sleep is another ancient remnant of wild dog-wolf behavior. It is not certain whether the circling served originally to flatten grass or to bend the spine before assuming the curled-up resting position.

The Leg Lift

You are probably familiar with the fact that a male dog lifts a hindleg not only to urinate in order to relieve his bladder but also, much more frequently, to spray small amounts of urine as scent markers of his territory. This territorial marking is just as important as the dog's sniffing perception of the messages left by other dogs in the same way. Allow your dog to follow this need when such behavior does not interfere with other persons' rights. Suppressing strong behavioral urges such as this may cause distinct disturbances to the dog's self-esteem.

Bitches are usually interested in this message system only before and during the heat period. Bitches urinate only to relieve themselves, not to mark.

Spaniels

Sensory Organs

While human beings do most of their orientation by sight, the dog is particularly guided by his extremely well-developed olfactory organ, the nose. A beautiful sight for a person may be of absolutely no interest to a dog if it has no odor. Conversely, we have a hard time imagining the complexity and excitement of a dog's world of scents. Despite specific other sensory qualities, the dog's primary guiding sensory system is his nose.

Eyes, Ears

The dog has the largest eyes of all pets except the cat. Though the dog's field of vision is much broader than that of the human being, his capacity for depth perception is more restricted. Dogs are naturally far sighted and are thus more oriented toward perception of motion. This explains why a dog may sometimes not perceive his master or mistress at a distance if the person remains immobile.

It must be said, however, that visual ability varies significantly from dog to dog. Amigo, for example, showed both excellent visual and superior olfactory abilities when compared to other spaniels. A specific case should also be mentioned: Afghans, Greyhounds, and Barsoi dogs have genetically higher visual abilities than other breeds. For their extreme running speeds they need better vision since their running would be hampered if they had to keep their noses close to the ground for orientation.

The hearing capacity of human beings extends from 16,000 to 20,000 hertz (sound frequency per second), whereas the dog's ear perceives 70,000–100,000 hertz. This enables the dog to hear sounds that are inaudible to human beings. A dog whistle sounds at about 30,000 hertz and is inaudible to hunter and game alike, but can be heard by a dog as far away as 1500 feet. This keen hearing explains why our dogs serve as excellent guards for us.

We also know and admire the fact that dogs not only can hear but also differentiate and remember a multitude of different sounds. Amigo proved this when we left him with a dog sitter during a vacation. Upon our return we found him standing at the gate, his head squeezed through the bars. Our dog sitter told us that, minutes before we arrived, Amigo had suddenly awakened from a snooze, ran to the door, and stood there, waiting, till we arrived, his head stretched toward the direction from which our car was to come. Amigo had doubtlessly differentiated the sound of our car from that of many others, and while it was still a great distance away.

Smelling, Tasting

The dog surpasses most other mammals in his refined ability to smell minute amounts of scent. This capacity is also his major guide for orientation. A dog can, for example, differentiate the particular scent of one person's perspiration in a million-fold-diluted environment.

Trained dogs, for instance, can discern single specific scents out of a multitude in

Understanding Spaniels

mixtures. Customs dogs serve to sniff particular narcotic drugs. Spaniels are highly suited for this use.

The ability to differentiate tastes is also well developed in dogs. This sensory system is closely related to the olfactory system.

Touching, Feeling

A highly refined nervous system allows extremely sensitive perception of touch and temperature. The most sensitive points for these sensations are the dog's nose, lips, tongue, and footpads. In addition, the special whiskers and eyebrow hairs heighten the sensory mechanisms of orientation.

Figure 32 *This is the way dog meets dog. After nose sniffing, they must sniff out each other's rump to establish proper contact.*

Meeting Other Dogs

A dog must experience contact with equals of his species in order to learn his own family system of communication. People who protect their dogs from contact with other dogs soon realize that the result is fearful and nervous behavior. This situation has often led to unexpected biting escapades when a sudden meeting forces the inexperienced, anxious dog into abnormal behavior.

According to good old dog manners, the first contact between near acquaintances starts with a nose-to-nose sniffing action. Once the two dogs know each other, they sniff each other's rumps (Figure 32), an action that leads to the major decision of tolerance (friend) or aggression (enemy).

Fighting for Ranking Order

In most cases you will find that two dogs are likely to show friendly signals, as indicated by their wagging tails. However, should you observe at such a meeting that a dog's hairs on neck, back, and tail are standing up on end, then you are witnessing a situation that will in all probability progress into a fight. At first each fellow considers himself the stronger, and their natural urge tells them both to show their dominance. It is not too late, though, to consider the situation carefully, lower the head, tuck in the tail, and retreat. If this option is rejected, a growling outburst and true fight develop. In most cases such fights sound and look worse than they really are. As soon as one of the contenders turns on

Plate 7   *Whether hunting or playing, the spaniel loves swimming.*

his back, offering his unprotected throat to the other, nature provides the winner with a biting block and the fight comes to an instantaneous halt.

Unfortunately, we must be aware that there are occasionally poorly bred or inbred behaviorally disturbed dogs that no longer follow the ancient "dog manners codex." These animals have been observed to bite even puppies or bitches, actions that are absolutely taboo in normal dog behavior.

Never try to pull fighting dogs apart. This can easily expose you to an accidental bite. You are better off with any type of distracting technique. Most dogs have specific reference words to which they react more strongly than to others. "There is a cat!," for example, has been used as a white lie successfully. Of course, a bucket of cold water is also quite effective—but unfortunately is seldom as handy.

In principle, it is important to realize that your dog is more inclined to fight when you lead him on a leash than when he is free. The dog accepts the leash as a connection to his leader and thus feels stronger and more self-assured—and overestimates his powers. The more frequently a dog has occasion to be with other dogs, the more easily he can deal with unexpected circumstances.

More frequent than ranking fights are practices that are intended to impress the other dog.

Impressing the Opponent

Trying to impress other dogs is also a pattern of behavior that ties in with the need for ranking order. Quite frequently, it is sufficient that one dog be impressed by the other's behavior, and a fight need no longer ensue to accept ranking orders. The opponent will be impressed by the maximum exhibition of a lengthened, tense body, hairs standing up on end all over, bared teeth, and a truly arrogant stature to appear as large as possible. The most inflated actor will win the highest rank and acceptance. This leader is usually already the winner, even if true strength must still be determined by battle.

Behaviorally Disturbed Dogs

The dog has become the animal most closely adapted to the human life style and behavior. The dog lives under the same environmental and behavioral stress factors as do human beings. Dogs are exposed to our moods and whims and habits, and are the victims of them. The same highly advanced human world is also a breeding ground for psychological disturbances. Increasing numbers of stress-troubled patients crowd the waiting rooms of psychiatrists. It comes as no surprise, then, that dogs too are occasionally seen with signs of neuroses and inappropriate feelings of aggression.

There are, however, a number of other distinct causes for canine behavioral disturbance:

● Poor breeding selection and failure to cull inferior genetic stock can produce undesirable behavior. Overemphasis is often placed on external appearance, at

Plate 8 *Playing, catching, jumping hurdles, and retrieving—the spaniel's activities seem limitless.*

the expense of physical soundness and breed-specific strength of characteristics. For some time there existed a line of red Cocker Spaniels that had developed a biting vice due to poor breeding selection and propagation of this trait. Fortunately, the awareness of modern breeders has allowed selective repression of the bad trait.

- Irreparable damage to the central nervous system can be caused by serious or prolonged illness. Distemper may leave a dog in such condition.
- Incorrect or no training, and humanizing behavior on the part of the owner, often lead to disturbed behavior.

Misguided animal love is the one important factor that you alone, as owner and master or mistress, can avoid as cause for your dog's ill mental health. Remember that you are your dog's pack leader and guardian! It is your responsibility to see that he is in good health physically as well as mentally and that he is trained to be well adjusted in the human society in which he is placed. In training your dog you should be as consistent as you are understanding.

A dog wants to be treated as a dog! To feel "dog-well" he needs a safe place in the pack, that is, your family and friends, and a recognized pack leader, who will act justly and can be relied upon for food, leadership, punishment when deserved, and love at all times. Humanizing behavior toward the dog is not acceptable in the pack leader! People who baby their dogs, spoil them, and treat them as toys must be prepared to deal with the neurotic dogs that

result. It should be mentioned also that continually changing life styles of the owner or continuous family feuds can lead to anxious, unbalanced, or distrustful dogs.

Aggression

When a dog suffers from lack of attention and from boredom, it may happen that his instinctive behavior is cumulatively suppressed; this, in turn, may lead to excessively aggressive behavior. As much outdoor exercise as possible, regular periods of play, and training are some of the best methods to prevent or reduce aggressive behavior.

Sometimes such aggressive moods can take strange turns, as can be seen from an experience our friends recounted. Their black Cocker Spaniel was tended by a friend during a 3-day business absence. The first 2 days passed uneventfully. Bimbo obeyed dutifully his foster mistress, whom he had known and liked well for a long time. As you would expect from a spaniel, eating was no problem. On the third evening, the woman left the dog in her apartment for 2 hours while she attended a birthday party. She felt anxious about her "house guest" and returned soon. Upon her return Bimbo responded with the wild behavior of hell's watchdog, not allowing her to enter her own apartment unless she dared ignore his wildly growling, bared-teeth threats. Calm talk and gentle persuasion served no end. The unfortunate woman was so frightened that she sat down to spend the night in front of her door, the dog on the jump. When the owners came to claim Bimbo in the morning, they found their friend dog-tired on the doorstep. Bimbo, jumping and wagging his tail with pride and pleasure at their return, never accorded his foster mistress another glance, or gave any further sign that he disliked her. Nobody could ever explain his strange behavior. Did Bimbo adopt his protective stance for the foster house because of the owner's sudden absence? Or had he expected his master and mistress and became angry when only their friend returned that evening? We can only assume that his aggressive behavior was due to the sudden confinement in a small apartment and the lack of physical exercise, and the occasion was an opportune moment to release some unexpended energy.

The True and Genuine Spaniel: Breed Characteristics

The international kennel organization is represented by all national registered kennel clubs, and it is on that level that breeds are specified and characterized. Spaniel breeds are briefly outlined on pages 14–17.

Most spaniels are closely related to the Cocker Spaniel. Cocker, Springer, Water, Sussex, Field, and Clumber Spaniels are individual breeds with specific traits; however, there are significant common characteristics: solid body structure, vivaciousness and intelligence, friendly and good natured dispositions, and marked ability to serve as hunting dogs.

The Cocker Spaniel is the most popular of all spaniels, and this dog is known particularly for his loyalty and affection and his penchant for fun and cunning. He adores children and has no inclination for fighting, provided that he is properly treated. Another typical spaniel characteristic is his dancelike step when he falls into a trot or is walked fast on a leash.

The spaniel has become the king of duck-hunting expeditions because he is singularly gifted for that role, and because he so loves to swim! By the way, a voluntary bath does no harm to a dog, provided that he can run about afterwards to get dry.

All in all, spaniels are exceptional hunting dogs, and it is quite unfortunate that so few of the breeds are actually trained and put to work in this vocational capacity. Luckily, there are numerous kennel clubs and hunting dog groups that organize specific exercise meets in order to promote activities in that field.

Let us add a few words on the subject of spaniel-specific care. The Cocker Spaniel needs daily care just as all long-haired dogs do. Part of that care is the removal of old, loose tufts of hair. Clip away curls that form around the tail. Also, remove clusters of hair growth between the toes and footpads, since these tend to collect dirt and impair the dog's footing. If your dog does not walk enough on surfaces that keep his toenails short, they will need a clipping from time to time. The veterinarian will show you how to do this, and then you can follow up on your own.

Trimming your spaniel true to his specific

Understanding Spaniels

breed requirements is not easy. You will do best to learn the needed know-how through your spaniel kennel club, since an experienced hand is indispensable. At first, while your spaniel is a pup, you may just consult a good dog-care center.

Certainly, quite some time must be spent on your spaniel's care. But what joy comes as a reward when just about everybody admires your animal—and the dog himself shows pride in his own beauty!

For the Cocker Spaniel, the measures of back length and shoulder height should be equal, thus giving the dog the typical squarish appearance. For all details of purebred spaniel characteristics, you should get in touch with a registered spaniel kennel club.

Bear in mind, however, that dogs, including your spaniel, are not custom-made—no matter how careful the selection! Not every dog can turn out to be Super-Dog. Only a few closely resemble the model spaniel idealized in theoretical descriptions. Because of subjective and wishful thinking, there are many disappointed owners when the dog judges have had their say.

Don't be sad if your dog passes as "good" instead of "excellent." Moreover, don't blame your dog; he doesn't have the slightest idea that he should be any other way. Remember: This spaniel of yours is still the most affectionate, loyal, and lovable dog-rascal in your world!

Figure 33   *You can participate in a dog show if your dog was bred by a reputable breeder, and if you have his coat trimmed according to kennel standards.*

Books to Enhance Your Knowledge and Understanding of Spaniels

Books about Dogs in General

1. *Training You to Train Your Dog*
   Blanche Saunders: Doubleday.
2. *Dog Care and Training for Boys and Girls*
   Blanche Saunders: Howell.

Books about Spaniels

3. *Brittany Spaniels*
   Beverly Pisano and Evelyn Monte, eds.: TFH Publications.
4. *How to Raise and Train a Brittany Spaniel*
   Edwin E. Rosenblum: TFH Publications.
5. *The Cavalier King Charles Spaniel*, 4th ed.
   Mary Forwood: Hutchinson (Merrimack Book Service).
6. *How to Raise and Train a Cavalier King Charles Spaniel*
   Elizabeth C. Spalding: TFH Publications.
7. *This Is the Cocker Spaniel*
   Leon F. Whitney: TFH Publications.
8. *Cocker Spaniel Guide*
   Hilary Harmar: Doubleday.
9. *Cocker Spaniel Handbook*
   Ernest H. Hart: TFH Publications.
10. *How to Raise and Train Your Cocker Spaniel*
    Evelyn Miller: TFH Publications.
11. *English Springer Spaniels*
    Diane McCarty and Janet Henneberry: TFH Publications.
12. *The Welsh Springer Spaniel*
    William Pferd III: A S Barnes.

Index

Italic numbers indicate color photographs.

Index

Puppy, choosing a, 11
Purebred dog, choosing a, 11

Rabies, 52
Ranking order, 61
Rations for special dogs, 36
Retrieving, 27, 42
Ruby Spaniel, 16; *20*

Scratching, 50
Sensory organs, 60
Sleeping quarters, 21
Smelling, 60
Sneezing, 49
Sporting spaniels, 14
Sterilization, 31
Stripping, 14
Supplements to commercial foods, 36
Sussex spaniel, *9*; 15
Swelling, 50

Tasting, 60
Teeth, 25
Temperature, taking, 53
Territory, marking out, 48, 59
Ticks, 25
Touching, 61
Toys, 27
Toy Spaniels, 16, 36
  English, 16
  French-Belgian, 17
  Tibetan, 17; *20*
Traveling with spaniel, 32
Tumors, 51

Urine
  blood in, 50
  dark, 50
  use of to mark territory, 48, 59

Vaccination certificate, 33
Veal bones, 37
Veterinarian, 32, 33, 48, 66
Viral diarrhea, 53
Viral hepatitis, 52
Vocal communication, 57
Voice, importance of, 26
Vomiting, 38, 50

Weighing the dog, 53
Welsh Springer Spaniel, 15